AF471068

STREETWISE FRANCHISING

STREETWISE FRANCHISING

Everything You Need to Know About Taking
Up and Running a Successful Franchise

Danielle Baillieu

Hutchinson Business
London Sydney Auckland Johannesburg

First published in 1988 by Hutchinson Business
An imprint of Century Hutchinson Ltd
Brookmount House, 62–65 Chandos Place, Covent Garden,
London WC2N 4NW

Century Hutchinson Australia (Pty) Ltd
88–91 Albion Street, Surrey Hills, NSW 2010, Australia

Century Hutchinson New Zealand Ltd
PO Box 40–086, 32–34 View Road, Glenfield, Auckland 10, New Zealand

Century Hutchinson South Africa (Pty) Ltd
PO Box 337, Bergvlei 2012, South Africa

Photoset in Linotron Times and Helvetica by
Deltatype Ltd, Ellesmere Port, Cheshire

Printed in Great Britain by
Antony Rowe Ltd, Chippenham, Wiltshire

British Library Cataloguing in Publication data

Baillieu Danielle
   Streetwise franchising.
   1. Franchising
   I. Title
   658.8′708

ISBN 0–09–173680–3

To
James, William and Sheila

Contents

Acknowledgements

I would like to thank in particular Professor John Adams, and William and Sheila Baillieu for their kind assistance and constant support.

In addition many thanks also to Tony Dutfield of the British Franchise Association, Michael Power of Power Research Associates, Martin Mendelsohn of Adlers, Peter Stern of the National Westminster Bank, Bob Riding of Franchise World, Roy Bishko of Tie Rack, Holland & Barrett, Wimpey, Harold Sorsky of M. Sorsky & Co., Chartered Accountants, and all the others who contributed so readily with information, and without whose kind cooperation this book would not have been possible.

How to use this book

The following method of working through this book will prove most beneficial.

1) Read through the book quickly to obtain a general idea of what franchising is all about.

2) When researching the franchise or franchises in which you are interested pay particular attention to:

   Chapter 3   Raising finance
   Chapter 4   Organizations to consult
   *Chapter 6   Researching a franchise
   *Chapter 7   The franchise contract
   Chapter 11   Other sources of information
   (*Work through in great detail)

3) Ensure that you work through the list of questions in Chapter 5.

Foreword

BY DAVID CHURCHILL OF THE *FINANCIAL TIMES*

It was ten years ago that I first started writing about franchsing for the *Financial Times*. Then franchsing in the UK was little understood by the world at large and especially by the media. If it was thought about at all, then it was seen as some sort of shady business activity akin to pyramid selling.

A lot has happened in the intervening ten years. The franchise business has seen its fortunes – and those of many franchisees – rise beyond all expectations.

But as franchising has grown in popularity and size, so it has also attracted problems. Any business which potentially can do so much good for both individuals and companies must be prepared to acknowledge that success does not come easily. Franchising has clearly been a prime target for attracting the 'cowboys' of the business world – those operators who see the opportunity for a quick killing at the expense of others without any regard for the long-term growth of the business.

Equally, some of the established companies in the franchise arena have also faced problems coping with their growth.

As an observer of the franchise scene, it seems to me that the industry is now getting its act together to sort out the problems it has faced. The British Franchise Association in particular has taken to heart the criticisms made of it and has acted swiftly and competently to tighten up its procedures.

But, in my opinion, there is still a clear need for books such as this one. Not only does Danielle Bailleu offer a clear and simple guide to the whole subject but she writes with the benefit of practical experience.

If her advice is taken to heart it may, of course, mean that the franchise business will generate less bad news for me to report over the next decade. I sincerely hope that this is the case.

Preface

The aim of this book is to provide a guide to the issues and problems that all franchisees face in business format franchising.

It will help anyone interested in taking up a franchise – from day one right through to when they have been running their franchise for some time.

A step-by-step procedure is followed which will shed light on the realities of commercial business. So often, franchisees are referred to as 'soft entrepreneurs'. This book is intended to ensure that they are well-informed, soft entrepreneurs. The key to success in any business is:

* **information**
* **good advice**
* **being in the right place at the right time with the right idea**
  hard work
* **a lot of luck**
* **and remember there is no such thing as zero risk, even in franchising.**

Franchisees do not have unlimited budgets and need to spend their money with caution. Professional advice is absolutely essential but potential franchisees can carry out much DIY research themselves in the initial stages. What questions must a potential franchisee ask himself, his family, other franchisees, the bank, the BFA, the franchisor? What information should a franchisee look for? Where can the potential franchisee go for information? How can the franchisee interpret that information?

The question and answers are given in an easily digestible form. Until now most books for franchisees seem to have assumed that franchisees don't want or don't need to know about finding out all the facts of a given opportunity. The author's experience is quite different. Most potential franchisees are enthusiastic, intelligent, hardworking people with enquiring minds who want to know *all about* franchising – the good and bad points. This book is dedicated to those people.

Franchising is a superb way of carrying on a business. It has its problems like everything else. There is no point in hiding the problems – indeed they are highlighted in this book. A potential franchisee has a right to know of the problems that exist and how such problems can be avoided or solved. All those who care about franchising take the view that potential franchisees should be alerted in such a way.

There are many good franchises – they sell themselves. They do not need artificial hype and unrealistic projections. The reader will be shown what to look out for. Would-be franchisees are taken through basic accounting principles that are necessary to any businessman or woman. They are shown how to prepare a realistic business plan and what the banks expect from them.

A franchise relationship is quite unique. There are many areas of law involved, some of them quite complex. The franchise contract is dealt with in such a way that the potential franchisee will be able to grasp the spirit behind the franchise contract and thus, be in a position to realize the implication of various clauses and the necessity for obtaining legal advice from the right people, *before* signing 'any contract'.

This book is also written for existing franchisees. It will enable them to understand their contracts. It will answer questions like: 'What shall we do – if we are having problems?' – everything is explained, from the new BFA Arbitration Scheme to what can happen if the business has to be closed down and how to deal with it. It will also prove useful to many professionals as a first realistic insight into franchising, although they will have to consult professional texts for more detailed material which is outside the scope of this book.

This book is a realistic 'down to earth' approach to franchising. It could just as well have been called 'Franchising, Warts and All'. The down to earth approach may not be welcomed by everyone involved in franchising but many professionals in the franchising industry who really care about the future success of franchising and franchisees share the views herein and have given unlimited time and support in the preparation of this work. It should ensure that franchisees are well informed in all aspects of franchising – an essential ingredient for ethical franchising.

1
Franchising as a legal concept

Franchising is not easily defined. The term is sometime applied loosely and even inaccurately to distribution and licensing arrangements, for example, petrol distribution and manufacturing licensing. You may come across the terms 'first generation' and 'second generation' franchising; these tend to be used by the US Department of Commerce. First generation franchises are the petrol service station and soft drink bottler types where there is a franchised dealer concentrating on one company's product line. The second generation franchise is the one with which you will be primarily concerned – i.e. business format franchising.

Business format franchising involves the franchising company (franchisor) granting a licence to its franchisees for a predetermined financial return (usually an initial franchise fee with or without future royalty payments). The franchisee is then entitled to a complete business package whereby the franchisor makes available to the franchisee:
1) **Expertise and market research.**
2) **Financial planning based on their expert experience.**
3) **Training.**
4) **Support.**
5) **The use of the corporate name.**
In theory the above should enable the franchisees to operate their own businesses to exactly the same standards and 'format' as all the other units in the franchised chain.

For those of you who want to delve deeper into the franchising realm the British Franchising Association defines a franchise as:

A concentrated license granted by one person (the franchisor) to another (the franchisee) which:
a) permits or requires the franchisee to carry on, during the period of the franchise, a particular business under or using a specific name belonging to or associated with the franchisor; and
b) entitles the franchisor to exercise continuing control during the period of the franchise over the manner in which the franchisee carries on the business which is the subject of the franchise; and

c)   obliges the franchisor to provide the franchisee with assistance in carrying on the business which is the subject of the franchise (in relation to the organisation of the franchisee's business, the training of staff, merchandising, management or otherwise); and

d)   requires the franchisee periodically, during the period of the franchise, to pay the franchisor sums of money in consideration for the franchise, or for goods or services provided by the franchisor to the franchisee; and

e)   which is not a transaction between a holding company and its subsidiary (as defined in section 154 of the Companies Act 1948) or between subsidiaries of the same holding company, or between an individual and a company controlled by him.

This definition may be compared with that of the International Franchise Association:

A franchise operation is a contractual relationship between the franchisor and franchisee in which the franchisor offers or is obliged to maintain a continuing interest in the business of the franchisee in such areas as know-how and training; wherein the franchisee operates under a common trade name, format or procedure owned or controlled by the franchisor, and in which the franchisee has or will make a substantial capital investment in his business from his own resources.

Comparing and contrasting the above two definitions show that:

1)   A franchise is a *contractual relationship* under which the franchisor grants a *licence* to the franchisee to carry on business under a name etc., owned or associated with the franchisor.

2)   The *franchisor controls* the way in which the franchisee carries on the business.

3)   The franchisor provides the franchisee with *support*.

4)   The *franchisee* provides and *risks his own capital*.

In many cases a franchisee is given a specific territory within which to operate and this will be stated in the franchise contract.

The franchise relationship has both advantages and disadvantages. Everyone considering a franchise must be aware of these and should weigh them up carefully and assess them in relation to their own experience and personality to ensure that they are suitable candidates for a franchise. All too often we hear that a franchise has failed because the wrong type of franchisee was running it. True, this can happen but it should be the exception rather than the rule. Make sure it is not you. Where it does actually happen – rare and isolated cases – the blame can be apportioned equally:

* to the franchisee for not assessing his own suitability correctly; and

* to the franchisor who should be an expert in everything relating to his franchise including vigorous recruitment procedures.

This reasoning has been put forward in many cases where large chains of franchises are experiencing difficulties. When considering such franchises the reader should be wary of a franchisor who habitually 'chooses the wrong franchisees'.

Advantages to the franchisor

Many people, whether they are established corporations or successful entrepreneurs, want to franchise because:
1) They can expand more quickly.
2) They are not using their own capital – it is the franchisee's money that is at risk.
3) They benefit from the economies of scale of bulk buying.
4) As they can build a chain of units quickly they are in a better position to get contracts than an individual.
5) Management of franchisees is easier because they tend to be highly motivated (it is their capital at risk after all!) and are even prepared to work anti-social hours in order to achieve success. It is not unknown for franchisees to work all the hours God sends for no salary when the business first starts up or until they are in a profit situation. Remember this could be you. You must be prepared for it, and if a salary is necessary it will have to be allowed for in the business plan (see Chapter 3) and will affect any borrowings you may need.

Advantages to the franchisee

1) The biggest advantage to the franchisee is that they can set up a business at a lower risk than with traditional methods. However, the statistic usually quoted – a 10 per cent failure rate in franchising, as opposed to a 90 per cent failure rate in ordinary businesses – is a fallacy. The risk is lower because the concept is proven and accepted by consumers, but it is not that low. Franchises can and do fail and the reader should always bear that in mind.
2) The franchisee benefits from the market research, support and training that the franchisor provides. This is ideal for those people who themselves lack ideas and technical knowledge in the field of the franchise of their choice. Indeed many franchisors will only recruit franchisees who have no experience in that field on the basis that they haven't picked up any bad habits.
3) Franchisees will be given assistance in setting up the business. Everything from finding a site, fitting it out and then continuing day to day assistance.
4) Franchisees will benefit from bulk buying.

5) They also benefit from advertising as a group.
6) One of the biggest advantages to the franchisee is the use of the franchisor's 'name' or 'brand', e.g. Wimpy.
7) The franchisee will also get preferential treatment from banks. For example, National Westminster, who have a specialised franchising unit (as indeed do many banks now), will lend up to 75 per cent of the investment. Banks rarely do this otherwise.

You should consider carefully the above advantages and weigh them against the following disadvantages.

Disadvantages to the franchisee

Even though a franchisee owns his franchise business he is not his own boss. A franchisee is often referred to as a 'soft entrepreneur'. Under the franchise contract a franchisee foregoes a considerable amount of independence. If you don't like being told what to do and you often have bright ideas – which may mean your unit being different from the other franchises in the chain – a franchise is not for you! The concept of franchising dictates the necessity for maintaining a uniform image. Your fantastic idea may be just what your customers want and a real money spinner but if your contract does not allow you to do it you won't be allowed to use your entrepreneurial skills – even when it could make a difference between making losses and breaking even. If you go ahead regardless you may find yourself being sued for breach of contract.

Most franchises require the franchisee to make continuing payments – called royalty payments – to the franchisor. After a period of time some franchisees feel that the payments they have to make are not a correct representation of the support and assistance they receive from their franchisor. In some cases the royalty payment will make the difference between the business making a loss or a profit. Some franchises may operate a two-tier royalty fee structure in which the more profitable franchises pay the higher royalty fee. This can lead to dissatisfaction between franchisees who feel that the system is unfair.

A franchisee may be restricted in the disposal of his business and normally has to seek the franchisor's approval. A franchisee may also experience difficulty in the renewal of his agreement (most of which run for five to ten years). There has been a case where the franchisor insisted that the franchisee modernize and revamp the premises before renewal – and after the franchisee had gone to considerable expense to do just that the franchisor still refused to renew the franchise contract.

In some cases the franchisor has decided that he no longer wishes to operate a franchise. The franchisee is left out of pocket, having paid a franchise fee and with no franchise – again his only recourse being to go through the courts which is a very expensive and time consuming business.

There is also a possibility that the original franchisor may assign the franchise to another franchisor. At present, this can be done without the franchisees' consent and could have dire results on the success of the franchisees' business. For example, the original franchisor could have had a staff of eighty five to support their franchisees (and this is what the franchisees expected when they took out the contract). However, the franchisor they assign to may only have a staff support system of three people! In such a situation franchisees may find that their business undergoes a rapid decline as they no longer have sufficient support to sustain the standards they have achieved to date.

A franchisee may find that the franchisor does not provide sufficient services, adequate stock or even enough advertising. At worst, his sales may be nowhere near the figures projected in the business plan and he may make hefty losses.

A franchisee's business may also suffer from mistakes, bad commercial decisions, misrepresentations or fraud by the franchisor. If the latter is true the franchisee may be in a position where his business fails and there is always the risk of liquidation or bankruptcy. In some cases franchisees have had to sell businesses and have still owed money to the bank. In most cases personal guarantees had to be given at the outset with the bank taking a second mortgage over the matrimonial home. In many cases the home has had to be sold in order to repay the bank. Thus, even though banks are willing to lend up to 75 per cent of the investment, it is arguable that this may not be such a good idea.

If possible, though unlikely, it is better to avoid personal guarantees, in particular such guarantees as a second mortgage on your home. Remember that the more under-capitalized you are (i.e. the higher your borrowings) the greater the chance that you will fail. For those readers who are now not so keen on the idea of franchising, let me hasten to add that providing you are well informed, realistic in your approach at all times, and careful in your research of the franchise it can be an excellent way of doing business, especially when it succeeds. A certain element of risk will of course always be present.

For those readers who think franchising is the ideal method of doing business, let me caution you to tread carefully and send off for the franchise packs which the franchises you are interested in will be only too happy to provide.

2
Entering into the franchise relationship

Franchise packs and glossy brochures

Always remember that the franchisor is basically a salesman. He is trying to sell you a franchise. In order to do this he has to convince you that:

1) his product/services are excellent.
2) he has carried out market research which shows that there is a real demand for the product/services.
3) he has a successful pilot operation.
4) turnover and profits are good. He should show you a specimen profit projections and business plan for a three to five year period.
5) the success of the product is due to his management expertise in that field and that you too could enjoy his success if he helped you with the business. Basically he is justifying the payment of the initial franchise fee.
6) if a royalty fee is payable that fee is worth the support and services he provides you with and that the business can bear the burden of the royalty fee and still make profits. If no royalty fee is payable and he merely provides a product then he will assure you that his markups on that product are the minimum.

Many verbal assurances will be given. He will be making all the right noises to reassure you. You have decided to go into a franchise because of the many benefits and support a genuine and ethical franchisor will provide. Those franchisors who are not ethical – and they do exist! – not to mention 'cowboys' will take advantage of that and will make empty promises. It is no more than hard sell. Do not be taken in. The people you will be dealing with are trained to be reassuring, well presented, well dressed, well spoken and to appear professional. Be wary of smooth tongues and the gift of the gab. All salesmen have them! Absorb what you are told and what you read – but do not believe a word until everything has been checked and rechecked and professional advice obtained.

A professional and ethical franchisor will welcome this cautious approach and all questions that must be asked.

It is worth remembering that sometimes a franchisor may not just make positive statements. He may omit to tell you some crucial facts. The ball is in your court and you have to anticipate where it is going to land and how you are going to make the return. At this stage it is vital that you keep an open mind until all research is carried out.

Many potential franchisees begrudge spending money on research and advice. However, it is crucial. Better to spend, say £100 on finding out that a franchise is not worth going into than losing thousands at the end of the day. No matter how small or large your investment it is *your* money and you obviously do not want to lose it. Even if you spend money researching several franchises it is still worth it and is certainly better than losing all your capital, being in debt, losing a year or so of your life in misery and trauma, and ending up on tranquillizers and involved in a court case!

Having read the glossy brochures the next step will be your appointment with the company. If you are particularly interested in a franchise you will go through several meetings with the franchisor.

The initial meeting

This will be an introductory meeting to give you the feel of the franchise and general details. There will be no financial commitment at this stage. If you are interested in a particular territory this may not be secured until you have paid the initial franchise fee. Do not let the franchisor hurry you. If you are very interested in the franchise then go ahead and carry out research on everything represented (see Chapter 3) *before* you pay the initial franchise fee and before your next meeting.

This is a good time to start writing down a checklist for yourself on the following points:

Yourself and your attitude to the franchise

Assess your desire, interest and capability to run the franchise of your choice.
– do you have family support?
– if unsociable hours of work are necessary can you and your family cope?

Professional assessment of a particular franchise
Put this into motion. See next chapter for details.

Examine the franchise yourself
It is very important that you meet other franchisees of that franchise.

The franchisor should be happy to assist you in giving names and addresses of franchisees *BUT* make sure you speak to whom you want and to as many franchisees as possible. Ask them:
1) How long have they traded?
2) Are they content with the franchise generally?
3) Are they getting the support and services from the franchisor that they were led to expect and are the franchisors as experienced as they say they are?
4) Did the franchise cost what it should have?
5) Is the product as good as the franchisor states?
6) Are they breaking even? } Are the projections that the
7) Are they making a profit? } franchisor anticipated being achieved realistically?
8) Is the royalty a burden or can the business easily support it?
9) Is the advertising that the franchisor carries out both sufficient and what he undertook to carry out?
10) Is there a franchise association? If not, why not? Would the franchisor object to one being set up?

You cannot ask enough questions, and it's always a good idea to ask the franchisor for a specimen franchise contract.

At this stage it would be wise to have an initial meeting with several banks. From your preliminary inquiries, you will already have a rough idea of how much finance will be necessary and how much you will require from the bank. The bank will give you some indication of their approach and how much they will be prepared to lend. Of course you will have to finalize matters when you can put a proper business plan to them for consideration.

When you have done all the above it would be wise to consider professional advice before entering into any financial commitment.

3
Raising finance

The banks' attitude to lending money for business is of course based on the viability of your business proposition, and whether ultimately you have enough collateral to cover the bank borrowings should anything go wrong. The banks will inevitably ask you for personal guarantees and will usually insist on taking a second mortgage on your home. If you need the finance you will have little choice but to agree to their terms.

The banks tend to take a more positive approach to lending money for a franchise than other business opportunities, and rightly so, because franchisees will be backed by expertise from the franchisor in a business that has supposedly already proved to be a success. However, any prospective franchisee should not get carried away by the amount of monies available – as mentioned previously, often as much as 75 per cent of the total investment – but carefully weigh up the franchise opportunity, methodically prepare a business plan and then approach the banks to see what they can offer.

National Westminster Bank

NatWest is one of the leading banks in franchising. It was the first British bank to appoint a manager to deal solely with franchising in 1981. Peter Stern is the senior of three franchise managers and a well-known figure in franchising. Over *£40 million* is lent to franchisees by the bank every year.

The franchise unit works by providing essential back-up information on any franchise to the local branch manager who is approached by the prospective franchisee. This gives the franchisee the benefit of a unique combination of specialist and local advice. The bank provides a specialist 'franchisee finance scheme' for established franchises; as much as two thirds of the total investment cost can be lent to prospective franchisees under the scheme.

The bank also provides a useful information pack on franchising which all prospective franchisees should read – it contains general information and more specific information on:

* small firms loan guarantee scheme;
* small business Digest;
* business development loans;
* insurance service for businesses;
and gives you guidelines on how to present your case to your local branch manager.

As NatWest has been involved in franchising since 1981 they have collated a wealth of information on franchisors and available franchises. You would be well advised to bear this in mind and to heed carefully any comments the bank is prepared to make.

The Royal Bank of Scotland

The attitude of the Royal Bank of Scotland seems to be very positive even though they were not prepared 'for banking policy' reasons to divulge how much approximately they lend to franchises per annum.

They provide finance for franchisees by way of a business loan/overdraft or both of up to 70 per cent of the total finance required. They are quite flexible and capital holidays of up to twelve months are favourably considered. They provide a booklet – 'Buying a Franchise' –which you should peruse.

Alan Auld, one of the franchise managers, explained how they operate. At the moment the bank is concentrating on examining franchisor companies and ensuring that they are setting up correctly. The bank also provides a booklet for franchisors – 'Expanding your business through franchising'. Mr Auld feels that by concentrating in this way on the franchisor company, greater protection is given to the franchisee. The bank asks franchisors a list of set questions:

1) What is the franchisor company's history?
2) Why have they decided to expand by way of franchising?
3) What is their ultimate ambition?
4) How fast are they intending to grow, and how many outlets do they envisage having in, say, a year's time?
5) What are the terms of the franchise contract?
6) What are their projected turnover and profit and loss figures? And what are their latest accounts?
7) How much do they need to borrow?
8) Do they have adequate management to run a franchise operation?
9) What problems have they experienced so far? If the company says none the bank definitely gets suspicious.

Most of the banks ask the above quesitons. So, in a way the banks are 'vetting' franchisors on behalf of franchisees. However, you should be aware that the bank is under no duty to disclose any information to you. No bank will want a potential franchisee to fail or invest in an unsound franchise, and while unprepared to make outright statements as to the undesirability of a particular opportunity, you should listen carefully to what the bank is prepared or not prepared to say! If, for example, they refuse to lend you the money for apparently no reason or ask you if you have seen the franchisor company's accounts – take the hint. Make sure you carry out the necessary research.

Barclays Bank

Again, approximate figures for the amount that the bank lends to franchisees per annum was not available. Barclays hands out an information pack containing various leaflets from accountants and is well worth reading. They also enclose a handout from the Department of Trade and Industry,

> Small Firms Centre
> Ebury Bridge House
> 2–18 Ebury Bridge Road
> London SW1W 8QD
> 01–730 8451

entitled 'What to ask the franchisor', a potential franchisee should read this.

In general, the bank will lend up to two thirds of the investment cost and in order to aid cash flow will consider a capital holiday of up to two years. The franchise unit provides a back-up service to the local manager who in most cases makes the ultimate decision. Some franchisors will have pre-arranged finance packages with the bank and in the appropriate cases these will be made available to the franchisee. Between £2,000–£500,000 available.

Midland Bank

The Midland Bank also produce a useful franchise information package which should be read. The bank stressed that it is left up to each branch manager to produce an attractive and competitive proposition to individual franchisees. Obviously, the branch manager has access to the franchise unit for specialised information. Up to two thirds of the investment is generally available, together with a capital repayment holiday of up to two years.

Lloyds Bank

Again it is useful to read through the information pack, paying particular attention to the questions which they recommend that you ask. Lloyds have a franchise business loan from which you can borrow any amount from £2,000 to £1 million. A capital repayment holiday of two years is available and the bank will lend up to two thirds of the total investment.

3 I Investors in Industry

3 I stands for Investors in Industry plc. Basically their function is to provide medium to long-term permanent capital to all types and sizes of business. They are an independent investor and currently have £1,700 million invested in 4,000 companies. Franchises are of course one of the many types of businesses in which they invest. They take a flexible approach in whether or not to invest. Much depends on the type of franchise, its size, how long it has been running, and of course the business plan put to them. 3 I never take a majority holding.

Unless very large sums of monies are involved it is unlikely that a franchisee will want to raise finance from 3 I, simply because it will mean giving away a slice of the business.

General considerations

As you will see most of the banks have similar terms for lending. All of them have a certain degree of flexibility, and you must ensure that you approach all the banks with your business plan to see exactly what they do offer. In theory they may appear to offer the same *but* in practice they will be different. One of them may have a special arrangement with the franchisor and will be able to offer you more favourable terms. Do not be frightened to ask them:
1)   Questions about the franchisor.
2)   What capital repayment holiday they can offer.
3)   What vetting procedure have they subjected the franchisor to.
4)   Their advice on whether there would be a demand for that franchise in that area. Remember, the local branch manager is in an ideal position to make such comments as he will be aware of how local trade is performing. He is also privileged with back-up information from his franchise unit.

But a word of warning – do not rely on what the bank says as gospel. There is no substitute for your own research and professional advice. The bank is there to help you and to provide you with an attractive proposition so that you bank with them and make money for them. A bank is a profit-making institution which will expect you to pay back the money you have borrowed plus interest whether your business succeeds or fails. Therefore, inevitably you will have to secure the monies you borrow (usually on your home). Given the choice, they would like everybody to do well – but unfortunately businesses do fail and it makes commercial sense to protect themselves. The information packs they produce should be read carefully and the advice they offer should be taken seriously.

The business plan

A business plan should be produced by a potential franchisee with the help of the franchisor and possibly an accountant. You will already have approached the bank tentatively with a rough idea of the finance you require. The bank will or will not have agreed *in principle* to allow the borrowings. Either way you need to go back to them with a detailed business plan which the franchisor should help you to prepare based on his expertise in that field. Some franchisors will only assist you with a detailed plan *after* you have paid the initial franchise fee. It is better to request that they provide the assistance *before* you commit yourself financially.

You will most probably have seen a hypothetical business plan for a given unit within the franchise network at one of your earlier meetings. The research you should have carried out by now will give you a realistic indication as to whether the franchisor is doing as well as he says he is and whether the business plan projections are realistic.

If the franchisor is based abroad his figures will be relevant to that country. It is crucial to ascertain what market research has been carried out in *this* country and whether there is a successful pilot operation here. Obtain all answers by the franchisor *in writing*.

Preparation of the business plan
Do not hurry over this. There is a great tendency for most franchisors to be over-optimistic with their projections, particularly understating costs – this will not help you in the slightest. However, if you have carried out all the research so far satisfactorily and your franchisor has survived the scrutiny, you may at this stage have some confidence in him. The franchisor's experience in the field of your choice will be invaluable and you will be able to rely on him heavily for guidance. Make sure that all aspects of the business are covered by the business plan including interest payments to the bank on borrowings, credit card charges, VAT, etc.

Note – Lease premium. This is a capital sum of money payable for the lease in addition to the rent. It could be a relatively small amount like £1,000 or it could be £60,000 or more, depending on the premises. A lease premium will usually be payable where the current rent under the lease is below the market rent. The difference will be 'capitalized' and will be reflected in the size of the premium the purchaser will have to pay. This is *never* included in the 'Cost of the Franchise' figure by the franchisor. You may or may not have to pay a premium. So, remember if you do have to pay a premium you may need extra borrowings from the bank.

What information do the banks require?

1) Start your business plan with a CV of yourself and your spouse/partner, giving full details of your personal status, i.e. age, married with two children etc., the jobs you have done and all relevant experience.
2) State the franchise you are interested in, giving details of the area/areas you are considering.
3) State the type of premises you require, e.g. primary/secondary, site and dimensions and approximately how much it will cost – bear in mind that a premium on a shop lease may be payable.
4) From information obtained from the franchisor and your own research give details of:
   a)   pilot operations and franchisee run locations of the franchise.
   b)   details of the market research carried out by the franchisor.
   c)   details of competition – particularly in the area you have chosen.
5) You should provide the bank with projected figures for turnover and profit and loss (which you have calculated with the assistance of the franchisor).
6) The latest audited accounts of the franchisor should be made available.
7) A simple cash flow forecast for the first two years should be provided, e.g.

Sources	Jan	Feb	March	April	May	June
Cash introduced						
Sales receipts						
Balance						

	Expenditure					
	Capital equipment					
	Formation expenses					
O	Start-up costs					
V	Rent-rates					
E	Fuel-heating/lighting					
R	Raw materials					
H	Wages, N.I. PAYE					
E	Drawings					
A	Advertising					
D	Insurance					
S	Sundries					
	HP, leasing					
	Bank interest and charges					
	Total outgoings					

8) When carrying out your research (see Chapter 6) you will have

calculated the gross profit, the gross profit margin, the break-even figure and the profit.

Gross profit = projected sales − direct costs (purchases & labour costs)

$$\text{Gross profit margin} = \frac{\text{gross profit}}{\text{sales}} \times 100$$

$$\text{Break-even} = \frac{\text{overheads}}{\text{gross profit margin}} \times 100$$

Profit = projected sales − break even sales × GPM

Overheads:
   Salaries
   Rent
   Rates
   Light/heating
   Telephone/postage
   Insurance
   Repairs
   Advertising
   Bank interest/HP
   Stationery
   Travelling
   Credit card commissions
   Sundries

You should mention all these in your business plan.

9) You should mention anything special that you have found while carrying out your research or anything that is worrying you.

10) You could make a brief statement of anything that your solicitor or accountant has stated.

Government loan scheme

It may be worth considering this scheme in certain cases. The funds made available by the government are limited. However, you will be able to submit your case and apply. If your application is successful then the government acts as guarantor to the bank for up to 75 per cent of your total investment. For this privilege you will have to pay a premium on the interest you will already be paying to the bank; e.g. you may have to pay an extra 2 per cent interest *above* the base lending rate. So, if your investment is £100,000 then the government guarantees £75,000 to the bank. If your business fails and you go into receivership the government will pay the bank £75,000 and you will owe the bank £25,000; if you have had to give the bank personal guarantees for the 25 per cent you will be liable to the bank for £25,000.

You should weigh up carefully the pros and cons of using the scheme. It is a big advantage if your business should fail. However, the cost of the borrowings become very high and may become an intolerable burden on your business.

Once you and your franchisor are satisfied that the business plan projections are realistic make an appointment with your bank.

4

Organisations to consult

Any potential franchisee needs to be very careful in approaching a franchise consultant. *Basically, there are two types of franchise consultants*: those offering advice to franchisees and for selling franchises to franchisees, and those offering advice to potential franchisors on how to set up a franchise. In both instances the consultant should be asked for a CV.

Consultants for Franchisees

Be very wary of anyone who purports to give advice on franchises. The question you have to ask is: 'What is in it for them?' In most cases you come up with the obvious answer: 'a commission'. Such consultants unfortunately do exist and are frowned upon by all those involved in ethical franchising. They may not appear to be franchise salesmen at first sight but you should be put on your guard the moment you start hearing glowing reports of a franchise for no reason. Good franchises sell themselves – they do not need hype.

The Franchise Shop Ltd

6 Old Hillside Close
Winchester, Hampshire SO22 5LW
0962 5530
Information packs giving details of franchises are available on application from the above address. There are only a limited number of franchises on the books but the information is provided without any charge to potential franchisees.

The British Franchise Association

It is essential that prospective franchisees are aware of the existence of

the trade association – The British Franchise Association (BFA) and
how it can help them:
> Franchise Chambers
> 75a Bell Street
> Henley-on-Thames
> Oxfordshire RG9 2BD
> 0491–578049

The BFA was formed in December 1977 by eight well-established
companies engaged in the distribution of goods and services through
independent outlets under franchisee and licensee agreements. These
were:

1) Budget Rent-a-car
2) Holiday Inns
3) Kentucky Fried Chicken   } of American origin
4) Service Master
5) Ziebart
6) Dyno-Rod
7) Wimpy   } of British origin
8) Prontaprint

The BFA aims to promote ethical franchising and to assist
franchisors and franchisees.

Assistance to franchisors

For franchisors applying for BFA membership the BFA lays down five
essential pre-conditions in its membership application form. These
are:

1) Members shall be actively engaged in the franchise system of distribution
of goods and services.
2) Members shall have established and be operating an ethical franchise
network which shall be based on sound business principles, and
providing a genuine and adequate service to both franchisee and
consumer.
3) Members will be required to demonstrate to the Accreditation Committee
the intention to provide, on a continuing basis, the service offered to the
franchisee and where relevant, to the public. The viability of the
operation, both with respect to the franchisee and the franchisor, must
also be demonstrated.
4) Members will be required to satisfy the Accreditation Committee that the
systems established by the member company are adequate to protect
both the public and the franchisee, where money is advanced in
anticipation of the service to be provided at a future date.
5) The member company shall give an absolute undertaking that it will
subscribe to the Code of Ethics adopted by the British Franchise
Association. This Code of Ethics draws heavily on the Code established

by the International Franchise Association and on the Code of Advertising Practice established by the British Advertising Standards Authority (A.S.A.). Members also shall have completed the following Declaration:–

We, the applicant company. .... Ltd give our undertaking that we are prepared at all times to subscribe to the Code of Ethics adopted by the British Franchise Association. We declare, to the best of our knowledge and belief, that the franchise system we offer is based on sound business principles and provides a viable and ethical business opportunity for the franchise and genuine end-product or service for the consumer. It is our belief that the systems we operate satisfactorily protect both the franchisee and the consumer and, accordingly, we hereby apply for membership of the British Franchise Association.

Signed etc. ....

Company and service information, together with references from three established franchisees must also be provided with the application.

Copies of current contracts and licences together with promotional literature must also be submitted.

A franchisor may wish to become a BFA member because the BFA receives inquiries from potential franchisees and of course, membership adds to the reputability of the company concerned.

BFA members are invited to attend seminars and working luncheons so that their franchisors are well informed of franchise developments. The BFA gives franchisor members advice on their franchises and also organizes exhibitions for franchisees to attend and talk to franchisors. A National Franchise Exhibition is held each year in October at the Kensington Exhibition Centre, London, organized by the Dresswell Group.

The BFA code of ethics

The BFA code of ethics adopted in accordance with clause 3 (2) (a) of the Memorandum of Association reflects the code established by the International Franchise Association, and is as follows:

1) The BFA's Code of Advertising Practice shall be based on that established by the Advertising Standards Association and shall be modified from time to time in accordance with alterations notified by the A.S.A.

   The BFA will subscribe fully to the A.S.A. Code unless, on some specific issue, it is resolved by a full meeting of the Council of the BFA that the A.S.A. is acting against the best interests of the public and of franchising business in general on that specific issue. In that case the BFA will be required to formally notify the A.S.A. setting out the grounds for disagreement.

2) No member shall sell, offer for sale, or distribute any product or render any service, or promote the sale or distribution thereof, under any

representation or condition (including the use of a name of a 'celebrity') which has the tendency, capacity, or effect of misleading or deceiving purchasers or prospective purchasers.

3) No member shall imitate the trademark, trade name, corporate identity, slogan or other mark or identification of another franchise in any manner or form that would have the tendency or capacity to mislead or deceive.

4) Full and accurate written disclosure of all information material to the franchise relationship shall be given to the prospective franchisees within a reasonable time prior to the execution of any binding document.

5) The franchise agreement shall set forth clearly the respective obligations and responsibilities of the parties and all other terms of the relationship, and be free from ambiguity.

6) The franchise agreement and all matters basic and material to the arrangement and relationship thereby created, shall be in writing and executed copies thereof given to the franchisee.

7) A franchisor shall select and accept only those franchisees who, upon reasonable investigation, possess the basic skills, education, personal qualities, and adequate capital to succeed. There shall be no discrimination based on race, colour, religion, national origin or sex.

8) A franchisor shall exercise reasonable surveillance over the activities of his franchisees to the end that the contractual obligations of both parties are observed and the public interest safeguarded.

9) Fairness shall characterise all dealings between a franchisor and its franchisees. A franchisor shall give notice to its franchisee of any contractual breach and grant reasonable time to remedy default.

10) A franchisor shall make every effort to resolve complaints, grievances and disputes with its franchisees with good faith and good will through fair and reasonable direct communication and negotiation.

BFA membership, registration and affiliation

The BFA publicly state the following criteria:

Membership
Franchisors are required to submit a completed application form, including disclosure document, franchise agreement, prospectus, accounts etc., and provide proof of a correctly constituted *pilot scheme successfully operated for at least one year, financed and managed by the applicant company. In addition, evidence of successful franchising over a subsequent two year period with at least four franchisees is required.*

Register of qualified non-member companies developing franchises
As for membership, including disclosure document and pilot scheme

etc., but with evidence of successful franchising for a period of one year with at least one franchisee.

Affiliate listing

This is a list of professional and other advisers who are experienced in the franchising concept and have carried out satisfactory contracts with existing BFA members.

In the case of franchise consultants affiliation requires them to observe a code of conduct prepared by the Association.

The BFA has used the slogan 'the symbol of excellence' and continues to advertise itself as the 'voice of responsible franchising'. Recent steps have been taken by the BFA to ensure that the above rigid criteria are adhered to and ethical franchising promoted. The code of ethics and criteria for membership etc., are very impressive *but* even so you should not rely on them per se. In some cases franchisees have relied on a franchisor member's status as indeed being a 'symbol of excellence' only to find that the franchise has slipped through the watchdog net rather than being caught by it. So in order to make sure that everything that should have been done has in fact been done you would be well advised to protect your position by asking the BFA the following questions and obtaining the answers in writing:

1) When did the franchisor gain member/other status?
2) Were the criteria for membership fulfilled?
3) Was the franchise piloted successfully for the correct period?
4) Were the correct documents disclosed?

    i.e.   disclosure document
           franchise agreement
           prospectus   request photocopies
           accounts

5) Have there been any complaints against the franchise?

The BFA declare that they accept the need for strongly perceived standards within the industry and therefore they should *not* object to you raising the above questions. After all, you are only ensuring that they are sticking to the standards they have themselves set for membership.

Unfortunately, whether or not a franchisor becomes a member of the BFA is purely discretionary. The recent Power Report shows that only about 25 per cent of all franchisors are BFA members. There are many excellent franchises that have not sought BFA membership. One cannot point to non-BFA members as examples of unsound franchises – indeed some of the best franchises do not belong to any trade organisation. So, it is important that you do not just consider BFA status.

So what conclusions can be reached?

In the absence of a mandatory vetting/policing authority, the BFA do a very commendable job. Naturally they have had their fair share of problems and criticism − fortunately all of which has been constructive. By 1988 they hope to have a training scheme for franchisees in operation. This will include courses in general business management, and the franchisor will pay for the courses. They are aware of the need to ensure that new franchises are developing correctly and ethically, and hope to have a new category of affiliate members who will be able to attend seminars and lectures.

The BFA arbitration scheme

At the time of writing this scheme had been in operation for only a few months. At that time it had not been used but the BFA indicated that its very existence had already led to settlements.

How does it work?
The scheme recognizes that in a dispute the franchisee is in a very difficult situation and may not be able to afford to take the matter to court. Under the scheme a franchisee will be able to refer disputes with the franchisor to arbitration, and even if he loses will only have to pay one third of the costs, plus of course any penalty or award the arbitrator may make. If the franchisor loses he will have to pay the entire costs. Only the franchisee can initially elect to refer the dispute to arbitration. The franchisor, however, has the power to refuse to go to arbitration and could take the dispute to court in the normal way. In such a situation there is not a lot the franchisee or the BFA can do. Only time will tell whether the scheme will work. A franchisor with any sense should not hesitate to take part in the scheme because it affords them the opportunity of settling disputes cheaply and privately.

The scheme will be administered by the Chartered Institute of Arbitrators. When there is a dispute the franchisee can contact the BFA and obtain a Request for Arbitration form which he must complete and return to the BFA with a deposit of £150. The form will be sent to the franchisor via the BFA and if the franchisor agrees to arbitration he simply signs the form.

The BFA sends the form to the Institute. An arbitrator is appointed and the franchisee has 28 days to submit written evidence in support of his argument. The franchisor has a further 28 days to respond. Written evidence should be sufficient. However, the franchisee or arbitrator can request an oral hearing. The arbitrator may request further evidence from one or both parties but it is envisaged that a typical case will take four to six months to resolve.

The scheme will also be open to non-BFA members. One of the major problems the BFA will face is to persuade members and non-members to use it. More information about the scheme can be obtained from the BFA booklet 'The Ethics of Franchising'.

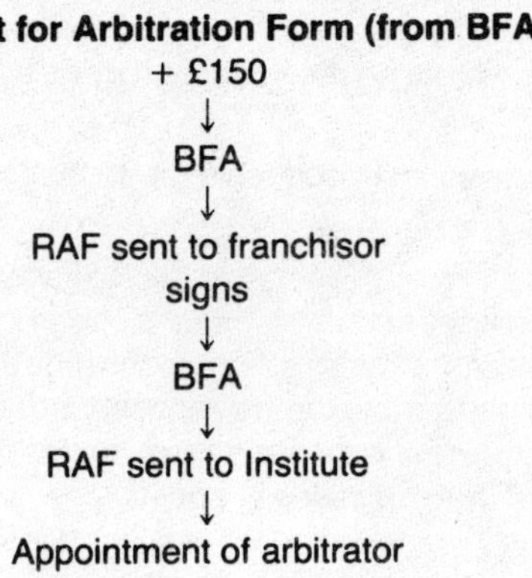

The Chartered Institute of Arbitrators/ BFA Arbitration Scheme

Application for Arbitration

To: The Chartered Institute of Arbitrators, International Arbitration Centre, 75 Cannon Street, London EC4N 5BH. Tel. 01–236 8761.
(To be submitted through the British Franchise Association.)

1. (Franchisee) ....
   of ....

.... Tel. ....
                                            and
(Franchisor) ....
of ....
.... Tel. ....

Hereby apply to to the Chartered Institute of Arbitrators for the following dispute to be referred to arbitration to the Rules of the BFA Arbitration Scheme for the time being in force for determination by an arbitrator appointed for that purpose by the Institute.

2. The dispute has arisen in connection with the following:

....
....
....
....
....

Note: only an outline is required here to enable the dispute to be identified by the parties. The Franchisee will be asked to submit his specific claim in detail as soon as the arbitration request has been accepted by the Institute.

3. We, the parties to this application, are each in possession of the current (1987) Rules of the Scheme. We agree to be bound by these Rules (or any amendment thereof for the time being in force that may be notified to us) and by the award of the Arbitrator appointed to determine the dispute.

4. A cheque for the sum of *£150 in respect of the Franchisee's deposit, and a cheque for the same amount in respect of the Franchisor's deposit are enclosed.

We agree to the disposal of these deposits in accordance with the Rules of the Scheme.

Signed (Franchisee) .... Date ....
Signed (Franchisor) .... Date ....

*Cheques should be in favour of: The Chartered Institute of Arbitrators.

The Chartered Institute of Arbitrators British Franchise Association Arbitration Scheme Rules

(1987 Edition)

These Rules provide an inexpensive and informal method of resolving disputes between franchisors and franchisees which the parties cannot resolve amicably between themselves. The Rules will apply to arbitrations commenced under the Scheme after 1 May 1987.

INTRODUCTION

1. In these Rules:
    (i) 'the Institute' shall mean the Chartered Institute of Arbitrators of 75 Cannon Street, London EC4N 5BH.
    (ii) 'the BFA' shall mean the British Franchise Association of 75a Bell Street, Henley on Thames, Oxon RG9 2BD.
    (iii) 'the Arbitrator' shall mean a sole and independent arbitrator appointed by the President or Vice-President of the Institute in an arbitration under this Scheme.
    (iv) 'the Franchisor' shall mean a company firm or person who is the franchisor in respect of any agreement under which a dispute arises and is referred to arbitration under this Scheme.
    (v) 'the Franchisee' shall mean a company firm or person who is the franchisee in respect of any agreement under which a dispute arises and is referred to arbitration under this Scheme.
    (vi) 'the costs of the arbitration' shall mean the total of the Arbitrator's fees and expenses, the Institute's administrative costs, and the cost of any independent examination under Rule 8(iv).
    (vii) 'costs in the reference' shall mean legal or other costs incurred by a party in connection with an arbitration under this Scheme.
2. The Franchisee may apply for arbitration under this Scheme as an alternative to court action. He must decide at the outset whether to use this Scheme or to seek his remedy through the Courts. If he uses this Scheme he will not be able to start again with court action, because awards made under the Scheme are final and binding on the parties.
3. (i) Application for arbitration must be made on the prescribed application form which may be obtained from the BFA.
    (ii) A deposit of £150 is payable by each party when an application for arbitration is submitted. These deposits may be refunded or may be applied in whole or in part towards defraying the costs of the arbitration, at the discretion of the Arbitrator.
4. (i) The application form should be completed by the Franchisee and returned to the BFA with the Franchisee's deposit.
    (ii) The BFA will then refer the application form to the Franchisor, to be completed and returned to the BFA with the Franchisor's deposit.
    (iii) The Franchisor's agreement to arbitration is necessary for the application to proceed. The BFA will encourage the Franchisor to agree, but he is not obliged to do so. If the Franchisor does not agree to arbitration, he is required to inform the BFA accordingly. The Franchisee's deposit will be returned and he may seek his remedy through the Courts.

INSTITUTION OF ARBITRATION PROCEEDINGS

5. Provided the application form has been signed by both parties and is accompanied by the appropriate deposits, it will be forwarded to the Institute by the BFA with the deposits.

6. The arbitration commences for the purposes of these Rules when the Institute despatches to the parties written notice of acceptance of the application. The notice sent to the party making the claim will be accompanied by a claim form.

PROCEDURE

7. *General*

Subject to any directions issued by the Arbitrator the procedure will be as follows:–

(i) The Franchisee is required, within 28 days of receipt of the claim form, to send the completed form, together with any supporting documents in duplicate, to the Institute. The Franchisee is also required to notify the Institute at this stage if he requests an attended hearing. (The Franchisee may not, without the consent of the Institute, claim an amount greater than specified on the application for arbitration).

(ii) A copy of the claim documents will be sent by the Institute to the Franchisor, who is required, within 28 days of receipt of the documents, to send to the Institute his written defence to the claim together with any supporting documents in duplicate. (The Franchisor may include with his defence a counterclaim in respect of any balance of payment alleged to be due on the contract between the parties, or in respect of any other matter notified to the Franchisee before the Franchisee applied for arbitration.)

(iii) A copy of the defence documents will be sent by the Institute to the Franchisee, who is entitled to send to the Institute any written comments which he wishes to make on the defence documents within 14 days of their receipt. Such comments should be in duplicate. They must be restricted to points arising from the Franchisor's defence, and may not introduce any new matters or points of claim.

(iv) The President or a Vice-President of the Institute, at such stage of the proceedings as the Institute considers appropriate, will appoint the Arbitrator, taking into account the nature of the dispute and the location of the Franchisee's trading premises. The Institute will notify the parties of the Arbitrator's appointment.

(v) The Arbitrator may in his discretion call the parties to an attended hearing, and shall do so if the Franchisee has so requested in accordance with Rule 7(i). Subject to that, the Arbitrator will make his award with reference to the documents submitted by the parties.

(vi) The Arbitrator will send his award to the Institute for publication. Unless the parties otherwise agree the arbitrators reasons will be set out or referred to in his award.

(vii) The Institute will notify the parties when it received the award from the Arbitrator, and will also notify the Franchisor of any costs of the arbitration payable under Rule 11. On payment of such costs, the

Institute will publish the award by sending copies to each of the parties. In normal circumstances the Institute will also send a copy to the BFA.

(viii) After publication of the award the Institute will return the Franchisee's deposit in whole or in part if so directed by the Arbitrator.

(ix) Unless directed otherwise in the award, within 21 days of despatch by the Institute to the parties of the copy award, payment shall be made of any monies directed by the award to be paid by one party to the other. Such payment shall be made by the party liable direct to the party entitled, and not through the Institute.

(x) If either party has sent original documents in support of its case to the Institute that party may within six weeks of publication of the award request the return of those documents. Subject to that, case papers will be retained by the Institute and may in due course be disposed of in accordance with the Institute's policies from time to time.

8. *Supplementary*

(i) Attended hearings shall be conducted in private at a place to be notified to the parties by the Institute on behalf of the Arbitrator, who shall use his best endeavours to take into account the convenience of the parties. The parties may attend a hearing in person or be represented by an employee (but not a person employed to give legal advice) unless the Arbitrator agrees they may be legally represented.

(ii) The Arbitrator may, through the Institute, request the provision of any further documents/information which he considers would assist him in his decision. If the documents/information are not supplied to the Institute within such time as it prescribes, the Arbitrator will proceed with the reference on the basis of the documents already before him.

(iii) Where in the opinion of the Arbitrator it is desirable, he may make an examination of the subject matter of the dispute without holding an attended hearing. The parties shall afford the arbitrator all necessary assistance and facilities for the conduct of this examination.

(iv) Where, in the opinion of the Arbitrator, it is desirable that independent examination of the subject matter of the dispute be made, an independent examiner will be appointed by the Institute to make such examination and a written report thereon. The parties shall afford the examiner all necessary assistance and facilities for the conduct of this examination and copies of his report shall be sent by the Institute to the parties who will then be given 14 days in which to comment thereon.

(v) If the Franchisee does not furnish his claim within the time allowed and does not remedy his default within 14 days after despatch to him by the Institute of notice of that default, he will be treated as having abandoned his claim. The arbitration will not proceed and the Franchisee's deposit will be returned less the Institute's administrative costs to date. The Franchisor's deposit will be returned in full.

(vi) If the Franchisor does not furnish his defence within the time allowed and does not remedy his default within 14 days after despatch to him by the Institute of notice of that default, the Arbitrator will be appointed and subject to any directions he may give the dispute may be decided by him by reference to the documents submitted by the Franchisee.

(vii) If a party fails to attend or be represented at an attended hearing the Arbitrator shall either make an award ex parte, or, if he so decides, adjourn the hearing for such time as he considers reasonable and serve notice on the party failing to attend that the matter will be dealt with ex parte at the adjourned hearing.

COSTS

9. The Franchisor shall be responsible for the costs of the arbitration less any amount which the Arbitrator may order the Franchisee to pay but the Franchisor shall in any event be responsible for not less than two-thirds of the costs of the arbitration. Where the arbitration is conducted on the basis of documents only, the Arbitrator will not order the Franchisee to pay a contribution to the costs of the arbitration in excess of £150 unless he considers the application by the Franchisee to have been frivolous or vexatious. In the case of an attended hearing, if the costs of the arbitration exceed £300, the Arbitrator may order the Franchisee to pay part of such excess in addition to the sum of £150 (or more if he considers the application frivolous or vexatious).

10. The Arbitrator may order the Franchisor to pay some or all of the Franchisee's costs in the reference, and may order the Franchisee to pay up to one-third of the Franchisor's costs in the reference.

11. The Franchisor agrees to pay to the Institute within 14 days of notice from the Institute of receipt of the Award and of the amount of the costs of the arbitration, a total sum equal to the costs of the arbitration less the amount of any deposits ordered to be utilised towards payment of the fees and expenses. This is without prejudice to any right which the Franchisor may have to recover from the Franchisee a contribution to the costs of the arbitration or the Franchisor's costs in the reference, ordered in the Arbitrator's award to be paid by the Franchisee.

MISCELLANEOUS

12. The arbitration shall be conducted in accordance with the law of England.

13. The Institute reserves the right to appoint a substitute Arbitrator if the Arbitrator originally appointed dies or is incapacitated or is for any reason unable to deal expeditiously with the dispute. The parties shall be notified of any substitution.

14. Awards made under the Scheme are final and binding on the parties. Subject to the right of a party to request the Institute to draw the

Arbitrator's attention to any accidental slip or omission which he has power to correct, neither the Institute nor the Arbitrator can enter into correspondence regarding awards made under the Scheme.

15. Rights of application or appeal (if any) to the Courts are as under the relevant Arbitration Acts provided that the special costs provisions of the Scheme shall not apply to any such application or appeal.

16. Neither the Institute nor the Arbitrator shall be liable to any party for any act or omission in connection with any arbitration conducted under these Rules save that the Arbitrator (but not the Institute) shall be liable for any conscious or deliberate wrongdoing on his own part.

The Chartered Institute of Arbitrators
International Arbitration Centre
75 Cannon Street
London EC4N 5BH
Telephone: 01–236 8761
Telex: 893466 CIARB G

Other trade associations

At the time of writing there appears to be only one trade franchise association in this country – the BFA. Although earlier last year an association calling itself 'The Franchise Trade Association' reared its head at certain franchise and business exhibitions, attempts to obtain information about this association and its activities were met with little or no cooperation. Nothing much has been heard of it since. Therefore without any tangible alternative you would be well advised to direct any inquiries to the BFA which at least has the reputation of promoting ethical franchising and can be seen to try to do that.

Commercial solicitors and accountants

Always remember that you must approach a commercial solicitor for information. No one would go to their local GP for major heart surgery, so why do people go to their local solicitor for franchising advice?

In the Appendix there is a list of commercial solicitors and accountants: it is not meant to be exhaustive and the list is given without specific recommendation from the author. For those readers who do not know a particular commercial solicitor it will prove a useful starting point. Remember that the Law Society at 113 Chancery Lane, London WC2 can provide you with a list of commercial solicitors throughout the UK, but again, the Society can make no specific recommendation on any firm of solicitors.

5
Preliminary enquiries

Once you know which franchise or franchises interest you, you should start making preliminary enquiries. You should ask:

* **yourself**
* **the franchisor**
* **other franchisees**
* **the banks**
* **and the BFA**

the following crucial questions, which will greatly assist in the analysis of the franchise opportunity.

Questions to ask yourself

1) Do you have the *desire*, *interest* and *capability* to run the franchise of your choice?
2) Do you have the family support?
3) If unsociable hours of work are necessary, can you and your family cope?
4) No business is risk free. Should the business not work for any reason can you and your family cope with the pressure?
5) What capital monies do you have available?
6) For the franchise of your choice how much will you have to borrow?
7) Will you have to have a second mortgage on your home – if yes, and the business fails, how are you going to pay it off?

Questions to ask the franchisor

You can never ask enough questions. The following is a long list but you would be well advised to work through it methodically and to record each answer. Set up a file on the franchise you are researching. By the time you have answered all these questions and worked through all the research necessary you will have a sound foundation for making future decisions:

1) Note the address of the principal place of business.
2) Is the franchisor resident in the UK. If not, where?
3) Are the trading and company names different? If so, what are they?
4) Does the franchisor have a parent or holding company?
5) Is the franchisor a member of the BFA? If yes, look at the questions to ask the BFA as well.
6) Has the franchisor made full disclosure to the BFA of the franchise contract and accounts for at least five years?
7) How long has the franchisor been franchising?
8) How many franchised businesses are they running at the moment?
9) What are the addresses of these franchises?
10) Can you interview other franchisees of your own choice? Look at questions to ask other franchisees.
11) How many company-owned outlets are there?
12) Ask to see the accounts of the pilots for the period they were run before franchising. Ask to see all the market research carried out.
13) What does the office organization consist of? Who are the directors?
14) Obtain CVs of all key personnel and directors.
15) Who will be dealing with you in the day-to-day running of the franchise?
16) How often will you see them?
17) Can they provide sufficient services, especially back-up services in the case of emergencies?
18) Have any of the key personnel/directors operated any other franchise business? If yes, give details.
19) Have any employees/key personnel/directors been convicted of any offence?
20) Have any employees/key personnel/directors ever been declared bankrupt?
21) Have any of the employees/key personnel/directors ever been party to a civil action for fraud or misrepresentation?
22) Have any of the above parties been involved in any other business that has become insolvent?
23) Which personnel/directors have been involved in preparing the projections?
24) If it is subsequently proved that any material misrepresentations or omissions have been made by the franchisor in terms of information and advice given to the franchisee, will the persons actually responsible for the misrepresentations or omissions hold themselves personally liable to the franchisee for loss, damage

and expense? If not, why not?

25) Has the franchisor been convicted of any offence?
26) Has the franchisor been a party to a civil action involving fraud or misrepresentation?
27) Has the franchisor been or is involved in litigation with a present or former franchisee?
28) Who are the franchisor's bankers?
29) Can you take up a bank reference for them?
30) Can they give any other references?
31) Does the franchisor have a special relationship with any bank in relation to loans for its franchisees? If yes,
32) Has that bank/other banks seen the franchise contract that the franchisor is offering?
33) Has that bank/other banks seen the franchisor's projections?
34) What finance is that bank prepared to lend?
35) Which of their franchise shops have had a turnover of people running them? How often? And for what reasons?
36) How many shops have failed? Where and why?
37) Has the franchisor bought back any franchises?
38) How much does the franchise cost? What does this consist of? Obtain a complete breakdown, i.e. initial fee, deposit etc.
39) What additional costs may be incurred, for example, a lease premium?
40) How much working capital is necessary?
41) Under what conditions is the initial fee and deposit returnable?
42) What recurring payments (of any kind) will the franchisee have to make?

Projections

43) What information are the projections based upon – pilot operations or
44) company shops, and what period do they cover? What size shop, which area?
45) Can you see the accounts that support the projections?
46) Are the projections based on a mature business or do they take into account start-up and development time?
47) How accurate have the projections been in the past?
48) Have any franchisees had to put in additional monies?
49) What was the discrepancy between the projected and actual cost figures in these cases?
50) Are franchisees attaining the turnover projected? If not, why not?
51) What delay period is there in attaining the projected figures?
52) Is the business seasonal – if so, what turnover can the franchisee expect in the different seasons?
53) When is the best time to open the business?

NB   Obtain professional advice. Interpret all the projected figures yourself, and with your accountant.

---

54) Is there any franchised or company shop which is trading unprofitably?

55) Ask to see a set of the latest audited accounts. Carry out the research on these figures stated in the book. Have there been any material changes since these accounts were prepared? What amount is spent on advertising existing franchises?

56) What amount, if any, is spent on advertising for new franchisees?

The franchise

57) Can you have details of the historical development of the business?

58) Details of the way the business runs presently.

59) What market research has been carried out? Ask for full details of what the research consisted of.

60) *PILOTS* What pilot operations were opened before franchising – what size shops were they and where were they? Were they company-owned? Ask to see audited accounts for all of them.

61) Will franchisees need to purchase any services from the franchisor or any other person affiliated to the franchisor? If yes, give details.

62) Is specialist equipment required? If yes, give full details of acquisition and methods of payment.

63) Is there any other equipment/machinery that the franchisee is required to buy/lease/rent from any other supplier? If yes, give details.

64) Are any such suppliers in any way connected with the franchisor?

65) Does the franchisor obtain any commission/'kick-backs' from introducing the franchisee to these suppliers? If yes, how much?

Advertising

66) Is there an advertising fund? If yes, what contribution will the franchisee have to make to it? How is the money spent? Give details.

67) How much, if any, of the royalty payments are spent on advertising with regard to a) advertising the franchise and b) advertising for new franchisees?

68) If a territory is allocated, is a franchisee confined to advertising within the territory?

The Property

69) From where will the franchised business operate?

70) Will freehold/leasehold/rented property have to be acquired?

71) Is any such property acquired from the franchisor?
72) If obtaining property from the franchisor, will the lease expire on termination of the franchise agreement?
73) How long is the lease?
74) What will be the permitted use of any lease?
75) Will you have to obtain permission for change of usage?
76) What are the provisions relating to rent review?
77) What rent will have to be paid?
78) Is a premium payable? If yes, how much?

Fitting out the premises
79) How much do the fixtures and fittings cost (including adapting the premises)?
80) The franchisee should be given plans of how their shop is to be fitted out. Who supervises the fittings?
81) Who pays for the plans? If the franchisee, how much do they cost?
82) Does the franchisor recommend builders/contractors?
83) Who oversees that the work is done correctly?
84) If the franchisor recommends that a firm of architects are employed to supervise the works, who pays for it and what does it cost?
85) In the past, what overrun in costs have been incurred?
86) How long should the work take?
87 *TRAINING* What training is given to the franchisee before commencing business?
88) How long does it take?
89) Where does it take place?
90) Who pays for it? If the franchisee, how much will it cost?
91) What additional training is given during the term of the franchise agreement? Who pays for it?

Restrictions
92) What restrictions will be placed on the franchisee in relation to the goods/services they provide?
93) If they can obtain goods from other sources, is consent necessary; oral/written? Is there quality control? Which other/if any franchisees do it and why?
94) Are there restrictions on a franchise supplying goods/services too?
95) Are there restrictions as to the geographic area in which the franchisee can sell such goods/services?
96) Is there a territory allocation? If yes, how large is it and how was it calculated?
97) Are there restrictions on advertising outside a given 'territory' or 'area'?

98) Are there any restrictions on whom the franchisee can employ?
99) What restrictions, if any, are there on what the franchisee/ employees wear on the franchised premises, e.g. is there a uniform?

Competiton and territory
100) How is the franchisee protected from other businesses operating under the same name?
101) What protection against competition is given to the franchisee from other businesses connected with or affiliated to or controlled by the franchisor?
102) What territorial protection, if any, is given to the franchisee?
103) Is territory allocation, if any, stipulated on a map? If not, why not?
104) What policy does the franchisor adopt if the franchisee obtains orders from outside his territory?
105) Can the franchisee advertise outside his territory? If yes, is consent required?
106) How are territorial disputes between franchisees resolved?
107) Can the franchisor unilaterally reduce the territory granted to the franchisee, if yes, in what circumstances can he exercise that right? Has he exercised it in the past? If yes, for what reasons?
108) If the franchisor can reduce the territory what, if any, right does the franchisee have?
109) In such cases does the franchisee whose territory is reduced have a right of first refusal to start another business in that same territory?
110) Where a territory has been reduced what effect has it had on that franchisee's turnover?
111) If an exclusive territory is not granted, how many franchises are permitted in a given area and how has the franchisor calculated this, i.e. what market research has he done?

Day to day running of the business
112) Will the franchisee have to run the business or can a manager/ manageress be employed?
113) How many employees will be necessary?
114) What will their wages be, approximately?
115) Will uniforms have to be worn?
116) What are the usual hours of business necessary to achieve the projections the franchisor has put forward?
117) Will the franchisee ever have to work longer hours?
118) Is Sunday trading included in the projections? If yes, then will the franchisor accept liability if the franchisee is prosecuted for trading on a Sunday?

Goods to be supplied
119) How frequent are deliveries?
120) Who pays delivery/freight charges?
121) What quality control is undertaken?
122) If goods are faulty, how soon must they be returned to the franchisor?

Read in conjunction with Chapter 6 on the franchise contract

The franchise agreement
123) What is the duration of the agreement?

Renewable option
124) Is the contract renewable? If yes, for what period and under what conditions? If not, why not?
125) Can the franchisor refuse to renew? If yes, under what circumstances?
126) Has the franchisor every refused to renew. If yes, for what reason?

Termination
127) Can the franchisor vary or terminate the contract unilaterally?
128) Under what circumstances can the franchisee terminate the agreement?
129) How many, if any, agreements has the franchisor terminated and why?

Sale
130) Can the franchisor assign the franchise unilaterally? If yes, what safeguards are there to ensure that the new franchisor offers the same standard of services that the franchisee originally contracted for?
131) Are there any limitations on sale/assignment of the franchise business?
132) Does the franchisee have to give the franchisor the right of first refusal? If yes, then is the open market value to be used?
133) Where the franchisee sells/assigns to a third party does the franchisor have to give his consent? If yes, what criteria does the franchisor apply?
134) Can the franchisor withhold consent unreasonably?

Death/incapacity
135) In case of death/incapacity of the franchisee, what steps will the franchisor take to assist?
136) What rights will accrue to the franchisee's next of kin?
137) What assistance will the franchisor give if the next of kin wish to take over the business/sell the business?

Restraint of trade

138) Will the franchisee be restrained from carrying on any similar business after the termination of the agreement. If yes, what are the conditions of such a restraint of trade?

Association

139) Is there a franchisee association? If not, why not, and would the franchisor mind if one was set up?
140) Does the franchisor hold regular franchise meetings? How often do they take place and where?
141) What system does the franchisor have for keeping in touch with franchisees?
142) Does the franchisor have a newsletter and/or hold seminars?

Company outlets

143) Where are all the company-owned outlets?
144) How do they operate, e.g. do they contribute to advertising; how do they pay for stock?
145) Do company shops provide the same goods/services as franchised shops?

Refurbishment

146) How often does the franchisee have to refurbish the premises?
147) Does the franchisor share some of the cost?
148) Does the franchisee have an option whether to refurbish or not?
149) Can refurbishment be made a prerequisite for renewal of the contract or an excuse to terminate the contract?

Franchise services

150) What assistance does the franchisor provide for its franchisees to ensure that high standards are maintained?

The operating manual

151) Who compiles it and how often is it updated?
152) Can you see a copy of the operating manual before you sign the contract? If not, why not?
153) Does it adequately cover all aspects of the franchise business including accountancy and book-keeping practices?
154) What is the VAT number of the franchisor? Are there any payments to be made to the franchisor which are subject to VAT?
155) Has the franchisor submitted a copy of the franchise agreement to the Office of Fair Trading?
156) If the business does not perform as projected for whatever reason what, if any, steps will the franchisor take:
    a) to find out why the business is performing poorly?

b) Will the franchisor give additional assistance in the form of management help on the franchise premises?

157) In cases of emergency/franchise holidays can the franchisor provide management backup services?

Specialist staff

158) If the business relies on specialist staff, e.g. computer salesmen, does the franchisor assist in recruitment?

159) How expensive is the recruitment process? E.g 'head-hunting' for a computer salesman is very expensive and can cost significant sums.

160) What turnover rate can one expect in such specialist staff?

Accounts and insurance

161) Is the franchisee obliged to have stipulated auditors for the franchise and can they choose their own?

162) If auditors are stipulated, who are they? Are they chartered accountants? What do they charge?

163) Does the franchisor have employers' public liability insurance?

164) Will the franchisee have to take out employers' and public liability insurance? If yes, are they obliged to use a particular insurance company? If yes, which one and how much does it cost?

165) In what way is the franchisee covered against claims by third parties against the franchisor?

Credit

166) Will the franchisee have to offer credit to customers? If so, does the franchisor have a special relationship with any of the finance houses?

Future growth

167) What is the growth rate the franchisor is planning over the next five years? Does the franchisor have the resources to cope with the additional growth – do they intend to increase their staff?

CAUTION

Obtain the answers to *all* of the above questions and go through them together with all of your other research with a commercial solicitor and chartered accountant.

Questions to ask other franchisees already trading/ex-franchisees

1) How long have they traded?

2) Are they content with the franchisor generally?
3) Are they getting the support and services from the franchisor that they were led to expect, and are the franchisors as experienced as they say they are?
4) What did the franchise cost to set up and was this comparable with the franchisor's projection?
5) Is the product/service as good as the franchisor states?
6) Are they breaking even?
7) Are they making a profit?
   } Are the projections that the franchisor anticipated realistically being achieved?
8) Is the royalty a burden or can the business easily support it?
9) Is the advertising that the franchisor carries out sufficient and in accordance with what he represented he would do?
10) What are supplies like – prompt/slow delivery?
11) Is there a franchisee association? If not, why not? Would the franchisor object to one being set up?
12) How good is the operating manual? Does it deal with all aspects of the franchise business adequately? If not, in which areas is it lacking?
13) Was training good/bad or adequate?
14) Is the contract fair? Was legal advice obtained before entering into the contract? Were variations requested? Were they successful?

Questions to ask the bank

About the franchisor
1) Ask them what they know about the franchisor.
2) How long has the franchisor banked with them?

About the finance
3) What vetting procedure have they subjected the franchise to?
4) What security will the bank require?
5) How much are they prepared to lend?
6) What capital repayment holiday can they offer?
7) What will be the bank charges?

Questions to ask the BFA

1) When did the franchisor gain member/other status?
2) Was the criteria for membership fulfilled?
3) Was the franchise piloted successfully for the correct period?
4) Were the correct documents disclosed?
   i.e. disclosure document
   franchise agreement
   prospectus
   accounts
   } request photocopies

5) Have there been any complaints against the franchise? If so, by
   whom and what was the outcome?
6)   Has any franchisee used or wanted to use the BFA Arbitration
     Scheme in relation to the franchisor? If yes, did the franchisor
     agree to it or not?

6
Researching a franchise

There are essentially two stages to researching a franchise.
Stage 1 – Researching the franchise opportunity and the franchisor company.
Stage 2 – Researching the franchise contract and the implications of all its clauses.

The first of these two stages will be discussed in this chapter. Stage two will be dealt with in Chapter 7.

The research budget

Many people think that research is a waste of time and they cannot be bothered with it. They often end up losing large amounts of money simply because they are not cautious. Make sure this does not happen to you. Anyone who believes everything they are told in business will never succeed. You need to check everything yourself and you need to obtain independent advice.

Research is cheap if you want to find a good business and you want to stay in business. When you have found a franchise you are really interested in it is advisable to allocate about 1 per cent of the franchise cost for research. For example, if the franchise is £45,000 then allocate £450 for research. This money can be used for obtaining independent advice from a commercial solicitor, an accountant and for carrying out your own research.

The franchise company

You must verify how long the franchisor has been franchising and how many outlets they have, including franchised outlets. It is also important to know what experience they have in that field. If the franchisor is franchising for the first time you need to know how many pilot operations they have, where they are, and for how long they have been running.

Market research

The value of market research cannot be stressed enough. It is essential that the franchisor has carried out a thorough market research to ensure that there is indeed a demand or niche in the market for the product/services that he has to offer. You need to know exactly what market research the franchisor has carried out. Ask to see the results. Note who carried it out and if necessary go back to the market researcher with queries. Note over what period it was carried out and what size sample was used. Do not invest in a franchise where no or inadequate market research has been carried out.

If you are given a market research report by the franchisor as proof of research they have carried out but you do not understand all its implications, then approach an independent market researcher for his opinion on the worth of the report and any conclusions reached, i.e. obtain a critical analysis.

Franchise turnover

You need to look for a low turnover rate. Of course, change in ownership could be for reasons other than failure, for example, selling or retiring, but, on the whole, a high turnover should be treated with suspicion.

According to Power Research Associates 6 per cent of all units of existing systems changed ownership in the last twelve months; twice as many as in 1984. One in seven of these changed because the business was collapsing; the majority were a result of a sale or retirement. Selling could itself be a sign of failure because another person may be willing to have a go where others have failed. You should request a list of every unit in the franchise together with *details* of change of ownership.

Failures

You must ask the franchisor for details of any units that have closed down altogether! Further, inquire whether the franchisor company has bought in any franchises themselves, as this could be a way of disguising a franchisee failure. According to the Power Report there has been an increase in failure rate from 12 per cent in 1984 to 14 per cent in 1986. It further states that where a business fails the prospects of a unit continuing are equal to those of it shutting down – partly due to the fact that where two individuals admit defeat there is a third waiting to have a go.

Apparently over 10 per cent of units at any one time will not be trading under the same franchisee a year later. This is twice the level of failure found in 1984.

Financial disclosure of information

You need to look at the latest accounts of the franchisor company. Ask for them, even if they have not yet been filed with Companies House. If sufficient information is not available for you to judge the profitability of the opportunity you are considering, you should not proceed. You must obtain the advice of an accountant specializing in franchising.

Projections
Treat these with caution and do not believe in them blindly until you can verify them by your own research. Remember they are only projections – that is, a set of estimated figures for illustrative purposes only.

The franchisor company

You need to ascertain with which company you will be signing the franchise contract. All your research should then relate to that company. There are cases where the franchisor company is a subsidiary company, i.e., a company within a group of companies. It is quite feasible for such a subsidiary to have little or no assets whilst other companies within the group have significant assets. You should ensure that the company you sign your franchise contract with is the one with the significant assets.

Directors
How long has the company been trading? The longer the better. Who are the directors and key executives? Do they have relevant experience in that trade, and in franchising? Ask the franchisors for CVs of the directors and executives.

Accounts
You should look at certified accounts for the company for at least three years. You may need to go back even further.

Court orders and settlements out of court
You need to ask the franchisor if there has been any litigation between the franchisor and its franchisees. If yes, then what was the outcome? In many cases settlements out of court are reached and you should request details. Everything must be obtained in writing.

Judging profitability
You want to go into business to make a profit. You need to ensure that the business opportunity the franchisor is offering you can indeed make a profit. Ideally you should ask to see audited accounts for at least three years of the pilot operations and satisfy yourself that they are indeed profitable. Of course, accounts may not be available for this

length of time. However, do not rely on just seeing projected figures. REAL AUDITED ACCOUNTS MUST BE SEEN.

The audited accounts can be used to project your own figures with the assistance of the franchisor and you will then be reassured that the projections are realistic.

Researching the franchisor company

A company search should be carried out by you or an accountant at Companies House, 55 City Road, London EC1Y 1BB. On payment of £1 you will be given a microfiche which can be examined there or, if you have access to a microfiche reader, it can be taken away and examined at leisure. You can also take photocopies of anything on the microfiche reader at Companies House.

Currently there are no postal search facilities at Companies House but there are many agents who will undertake a search for you for a fee, e.g. Jordan & Sons Ltd, Jordan House, 47 Brunswick Place, London N1 6EE. Don't forget to ask the franchisor the name of the company as it may be different from the trading name.

The directors' report

This will contain:
* Information required by law.
* Information required by the Stock Exchange (where the company is quoted).
* Voluntary information.

Statutory requirements

Under the Companies Act 1985 a director's report must give the following information:

1) The principal activities of the company and its subsidiaries and any significant change – Section 235.
2) A fair review of the development of the business during the year together with an indication of future developments and research and development activities – Section 235 and Schedule 7, paras 6b and c. However, in practice you will find only the briefest of comments.
3) The names of the directors and details of their shareholdings – Schedule 7, paragraph 2.
4) Particulars of significant changes in fixed assets – Schedule 7, page 1.
5) Details of the company's shares acquired by the company itself during the year – Schedule 7, part 11.
6) Important events affecting the company which have occurred since the end of the year.
7) Statement of political or charitable contributions if over £200 per annum.

Stock exchange requirements
1) A geographical analysis of turnover of operations outside the UK
   and Ireland is required, and what this turnover contributes to the
   trading results if that contribution is abnormal in any way.
2) Details of anyone other than directors who hold 5 per cent or more
   shares of the class of voting capital.
3) Whether the company is 'closed' or not.

Chairman's statement
This may or may not be present. If present, it will contain comments on
a number of general things, e.g., company strategy and plans for the
future. Be cautious when reading it and always remember that it is the
chairman's job to maintain confidence in the company and therefore
he will be concentrating on the good points.

Auditors' report
Every company has to appoint an auditor at each annual general
meeting (AGM). Under the Companies Act 1985 it is an offence for a
director or company secretary to give false or misleading information
to auditors. The auditors have to report to the shareholders whether in
their opinion the profit and loss account and the balance sheet and any
group accounts have been properly prepared, and that they give a true
and fair view of the profit and state of affairs of the company or group.
Thus, it is important for you to take note of what the auditor says. If the
auditor thinks proper accounting records have not been kept or if they
cannot obtain necessary information they must 'qualify' their report. If
the accounts of the franchisor company are qualified in any way, seek
independent professional advice immediately before proceeding any
further.

Information from other sources

The main sources of information are of course the annual report and
the accounts. However, there are a number of other sources of
information which will give you a more complete picture of the
company. These are:

Quarterly or half yearly reports
Such interim statements are not audited but are useful.

Prospectuses
A prospectus must be issued by a company when it offers shares or
debentures for sale to the general public. The Third Schedule of
Companies Act 1985 lays down the items that must be contained in the
prospectus. Furthermore, when a company goes 'public', i.e. its shares

have a listing on the Stock Exchange, the prospectus has to include information for listing. Thus, the prospectus contains a lot of really useful information – this is usually as follows:
* Details of the offer, share capital, and how much has been borrowed.
* Details of directors, company secretary, auditors, financial advisors, solicitors, stockbrokers and bankers.
* Description of the company
  - history
  - business description
  - details on management and staff
  - company premises
  - where new shares are being issued a statement saying how proceeds will be used
  - forecast of year's profits, details of dividends
  - future prospects and plans for the company
* The accountant's report – profit and loss accounts, source and application of funds over three years and the latest balance sheets.
* General information, e.g. directors' interests, pending litigation.
* Statutory information.

Circulars

For quoted public companies which are subject to the rules of the Stock Exchange. The yellow book, section 6, divides transactions into four classes. Depending on which class the transaction falls into rules are set down as to what the company is required to do, e.g. Class 1.

> Company is required to make an announcement to the Company Announcements Office and to the Press, *AND* must send out a circular to shareholders (and obtain their consent if necessary) *OR* publish listings particulars (if no consent is required).

The information in circulars is very useful as it will give you details of any major additions to, or realizations of the company's assets.

Newsletters and magazines

Many companies produce magazines or newsletters for their employees once a year. These can be very useful, if you can get your hands on them, as they may contain information that is not in the accounts. Some companies will make newsletters and magazines available to shareholders as well. They may even be distributed more frequently.

Sales information

Look at all the promotional literature of the company. It will give you an insight into, for example, its pricing, policy and the quality of its product range.

Documents issued in a contested bid
If you are interested in a franchisor company which has successfully defended a bid then it will be useful to look at the documents which were issued in defence of the bid, because the company will have been fighting for its independence and will have been more forthcoming about its future plans.

The profit and loss account

What it looks like.

Example

The profit and loss account. For the year ending 31.12.86.

1)	*Sales turnover*		£150,000
	Opening stock	10,000	
	Purchases	45,000	
	Closing stock	15,000	
2)	− Cost of sales (opening stock+purchases−closing stock)		40,000
3)	= Gross profit (sales+closing stock−opening stock+ purchases)		110,000
4)	− Expenses		90,000
5)	= Operating profit		20,000
6)	− Interest charges		5,000
7)	= Profit before tax		15,000
8)	− Taxation		4,000
9)	= Profit after tax		11,000
10)	− Dividends		4,000
11)	= Profit retained		7,000

Points to note
The date − note this carefully, as it shows what time period the accounts cover.
1) *Sales turnover* – this is the total income that you receive into the business.
2) *Cost of sales* – This is obtained by adding the opening stock to the purchases and then deducting the closing stock.
3) *Gross profit* – Sales Turnover – Cost of Sales (but before overheads). This figure will give you an indication of how efficiently the business is run.
4) *Expenses* – These are all the costs incurred in selling the product or service. For example:
   +business salaries (including own drawings)

+ Rent
+ Rates
+ Lighting/heating
+ telephone/postage
+ insurance
+ repairs
+ advertising
+ bank interest
+ other expenses   _________
= Total overheads   _________

5) Operating profit = gross profit − expenses.
6) *Interest charges* These could be a major expense depending upon how much has been borrowed.
   Operating profit − interest charges = profit before tax.
7) Tax can then be deducted to give you profit after tax and dividends can then be deducted to leave you with retained profits.

You need to work your way through the companies' profit and loss accounts over at least a three year period. Certain key profitability ratios will be useful in interpretation of the accounts, and will be discussed later. Next you need to look at the companies' balance sheet.

The balance sheet

Balance Sheet as at 31.12.86

Capital £	*Fixed assets*
Cash introduced on	Land and buildings
	Machinery
	Motor vehicles
+ Net profit for the year	*Current assests*
Drawings	Stock
	Debtors
	Bank
	Cash
Current liabilities	
Trade creditors	
Accrued expenses	

Notes
The balance sheet is a statement of the company at a particular moment in time − so again, you need to note the date. The balance sheet is divided into two sections. The assets of the business on one side and on the other side what the business is financed by, i.e. liabilities.

The two sides have to balance as a business can only have assets to the value of what it has invested in the business.

The working capital is calculated by subtracting current liabilities from current assets, i.e.

current assets − current liabilities = working capital

The working capital represents money immediately tied up in the business. The money that is needed to finance the working capital is often called net current assets in the balance sheet, although at other times the term working capital tends to be used.

Capital

This can be from three sources:
* share capital
* profit/loss from previous years
* loan capital – e.g. from a bank.

Overdraft from bank

This would be treated as a current liability. Interest will be payable on the overdraft and will have to be repaid whether or not the business is successful.

There are two types of assets – fixed and current. They are usually listed starting with the most permanent asset, i.e. *fixed assets*, the one most difficult to turn into cash progressing to the one most easily turned into cash. These are such things as the premises, business and machinery. Basically they are assets of the company which will be assets over a long period of time. *Current assets* are assets that represent cash or are mainly used for conversion into cash and they usually have a short life. As in the example they are such things as stock, debtors, bank and cash.

It is absolutely essential for anyone going into a business not only to look at the above financial reports but to interpret the accounts using key ratios or to consult an accountant to do the same. You need to ensure that the business is financially sound and that you will make a good profit.

Use of key ratios

Three types of ratio will be discussed:
1) Operating ratios – these show how the company is trading.
2) Financial ratios – these measure the financial structure of a company and relate to the company's trading activities.
3) Investment ratios – relate the number of ordinary shares and their market price to the profits, dividends and assets of the company.

We shall be concentrating on the first two types of ratio.

1)

$$\frac{\text{trading profit}}{\text{turnover (sales)}} \times 100 \text{ gives profit margin on sales}$$

trading profit = profit before interest charges and tax.

In a manufacturing industry the profit margin on sales is between 8 per cent and 10 per cent, while in food retailing it is about 3 per cent because dealing in high volumes and low margins.
Note: Profit margin on sales is *not* the same as gross profit margin.

If the profit margin on sales is *low* it is a sign of poor performance. What you need to look for is better than average margins which will indicate good management within the company.

2)

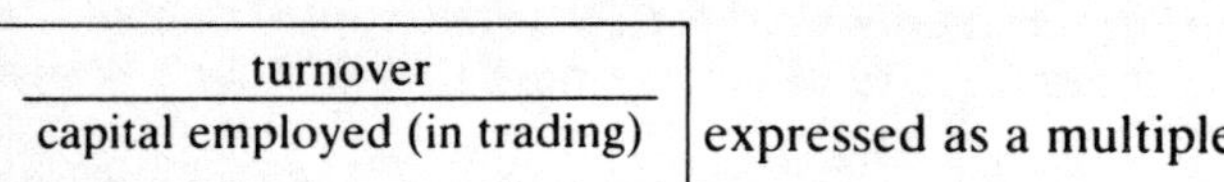

$$\frac{\text{trading profit}}{\text{capital employed}} \times 100 = \text{return on capital employed (ROCE)}$$

This is one of the most important ratios as a measure of profitability. The ROCE can be calculated for the company or any of its trading activities; if it is very low for any part of the business then this suggests that activity should not be continued unless obviously an integral part of the business. When the ROCE is very low the company should also be wary of starting new activities.

3)

$$\frac{\text{turnover}}{\text{capital employed (in trading)}} \quad \text{expressed as a multiple}$$

An increase in this ratio indicates improvement in performance but if the ratio is increasing too rapidly watch out! It could be a sign of overtrading.

4)

$$\frac{\text{stocks}}{\text{turnover}} \times 100$$

A well-run company usually tries to carry the minimum stock needed, simply because they will not want money tied up unnecessarily. A rising stock ratio without any reason reflects lack of demand for the goods and/or poor stock control. An average manufacturing company should have a stocks/turnover ratio of around 25 to 30 per cent.

5)

$$\boxed{\dfrac{\text{trade debtors}}{\text{turnover}}}$$ expressed as a percentage or multiplied by 365, as the collection period in days

Normal terms of payments for most companies are at the end of the month following delivery. The average credit given would be about six to seven weeks, making debtors about 12 per cent of turnover. Realistically, a debtors' figure of 20 to 28 per cent is quite normal, although some companies do give longer credit to be more competitive. A decreasing collection period may at first appear to be a good sign but you need to verify that the company is not just desperate for cash and exerting undue pressure on customers or giving extra discounts for cash.

6)

$$\boxed{\dfrac{\text{trade creditors}}{\text{sales}} \times 100}$$

This ratio indicates the amount of credit the company is allowed by its suppliers. It is a very useful ratio to monitor because the suppliers are closest to the company. If you see that the company is trying to get as much credit as it can despite forfeiting on discounts it shows that it is short of cash. Be especially wary of the company changing suppliers – it is usually a good warning signal.

7)

$$\boxed{\dfrac{\text{working capital}}{\text{sales}} \times 100}$$ working capital = (stocks and trade debtors − trade creditors)

This ratio shows how much capital is needed to finance operations in addition to capital invested in fixed assets. This ratio can vary vastly but if it drops you should be wary because the company may be overtrading.

In addition to analysing the above ratios you should be aware of the following financial ratios which can prove very informative. You need to ensure that the franchisor company is not 'over geared', i.e. that it has not borrowed so much (compared to equity) that it has an adverse effect on the business. You will also need to ensure that you are not overgeared when you set up your franchise. Interest paid to service borrowings is profit foregone.

8)

$$\boxed{\dfrac{\text{debt}}{\text{equity}} \times 100}$$ A good ratio to check on

When setting up the borrowings for your franchise your gearing should be no more than 50 per cent. This will alleviate pressures on the business. In many cases banks will be prepared to lend up to 75 per cent, but be careful to ensure that the business can support the borrowings.

You will need to assess the franchisor companies' liquidity. You can do this by looking at the companies within the franchisor group of companies.

9)

$$\text{current ratio} = \frac{\text{current assets}}{\text{current liabilities}}$$

This ratio can vary widely depending on the type of business but generally a current ratio of between 1·5 to 2 is regarded as normal. Any lower ratio is a warning sign.

Another ratio to consider here would be what is called the quick ratio or acid test.

10)

$$\text{acid test} = \frac{\text{current assets} - \text{stock}}{\text{current liabilities}}$$

This ratio is very important because it recognizes that a certain amount of the current assets are tied up in stock and cannot be readily converted to cash. If the company was put into a situation where it had to settle with its creditors by collecting immediately from its debtors this ratio will indicate whether the company can indeed do that. If the ratio is less than 1 then the company will not be able to settle.

Cash flow can be the biggest problem in a business. If the above ratios cause concern the company might be having cash flow problems and you will need to investigate the matter in more detail. If the company is experiencing cash flow problems it will eventually run into an overtrading situation unless it rectifies the problem – which it can do in a number of ways. You need to establish whether or not the problem exists and if it does exist that the company is dealing with it effectively. Remember that cash flow difficulties experienced by the franchisor will adversely affect its franchisees, e.g. reduced advertising, limited new stock.

It is not suggested that you should laboriously work through all the above ratios. But, you must be aware of the depth of research that is absolutely necessary before you invest your monies. It would be very useful to follow the above guidelines for example where you are interested in several franchise opportunities. Carry out your own DIY research on all of them and after you have eliminated some (which is a certainty) approach a commercial accountant for an independent, professional analysis. If the franchisor company is sound you can continue.

The franchisor will provide you with projected figures (which are based on the pilot operations and other franchises) and you will have to research all the above points in relation to what is being offered to you:

Research profit and loss account $\rbrace$ using the projected figures
balance sheet $\rbrace$ and key ratios

You need to ensure that the projected figures are realistic and that business can be profitable. You must contact all existing franchisees and ask them whether they are making a profit. Ask to see their accounts – they may oblige. Do not take anything on trust. You should calculate the following:

1) *Your gross profit*

Projected sales − direct costs = gross profit (purchases, labour costs)

e.g.   £100,000 − (£20,000 + £30,000) = £50,000 GP

2) *Your gross profit margin*

GPM = $\dfrac{\text{gross profit}}{\text{sales}} \times 100$

e.g.   GPM = $\dfrac{50,000 \times 100}{100,000} = 50\%$

3) *Your overheads or expenses* – (see list on page 48)
For example, take them as being £30,000 in this case and then you can calculate your breakeven point.

4) *Your breakeven*

$\dfrac{\text{overheads}}{\text{gross profit margin}} \times 100 = \text{breakeven}$

e.g. $\dfrac{30,000 \times 100}{50} = 60,000$

   i.e.   £60,000 is needed just to break even.

The monthly breakeven can be calculated by simply dividing the breakeven sales by 6 if projections are for 6 months (as here) or 12 if they are annual projections.

e.g. $\dfrac{60,000}{6} = 10,000$

So, in this example £10,000 is needed per month just to break even. Anything above this will be a profit. If the business is unable to generate a minimum of £10,000 per month it will be trading at a loss and will be unable to meet liabilities.

Before you start in business you need to ensure that the level of sales needed to break even is indeed realistic, and when you are trading you will need to monitor the sales and the breakeven continuously and regularly. Remember that your breakeven calculations will give you an average monthly or weekly breakeven target, but in practice actual sales can fluctuate due to seasonal differences.

5) *Profit*

Projected sales − breakeven sales × gross profit = profit margin

e.g.   100,000 − 60,000 × 50% = 20,000
  Profit = £20,000 for six months in this example.

The calculations above are essential, not only for analysing the franchise opportunity but for inclusion in your business plan and presentation to your bank manager. Discuss all projections with an accountant and make sure that they are advisable for the location you are considering.

Remember: 'RESEARCH IS A BLIND DATE WITH KNOW-LEDGE'. You do not know what you will find. You should research with an open mind. Be prepared for anything. Your research may show that it is not worth investing in the venture – heed the facts and figures you have found and do not go ahead regardless because you have a 'hunch' that it will work. In such a case your research will have saved you from investing in a bad business opportunity.

On the other hand your research may be very positive and you will be able to invest with confidence. Always remember, however, that no business is risk free.

7

The franchise contract

Once you have researched and assessed the franchise opportunity and satisfied yourself that the franchisor's claims are realistic and achievable you need to *research and understand* the franchise contract and the implications of the terms.

No reputable franchisor is out to score points or gain an unfair advantage over you in the agreement, *but remember* that the franchisor and his advisors have written the agreement – so it is bound to favour his interests rather than yours. The balance of doubt is *not* on your side and the scales are tipped in his favour. It is up to you to make sure you even the odds.

The franchise contract is traditionally regarded as non-negotiable. The reason being that the foundation of the franchise concept is strict uniformity between outlets. This is absolutely correct. But there is no reason why all the franchisees in a chain cannot have the same equitable and fair contract. You have to stand firm in trying to get what is best for you. Don't put up with unfair clauses. Get your solicitor to negotiate on terms that are a problem. If you get no joy from the franchisor don't proceed any further. If enough franchisees make it clear that they won't settle for the unfair contracts that can and do exist the franchisor will eventually have to play ball fairly or not play ball at all. It's up to you. *Remember* – the contract is the only formal, legally binding agreement that you will have. The terms within it are vital. It will govern every aspect of your franchise relationship. (A specimen franchise contract is given at the end of this chapter.)

The CONTRACT begins with a statement of the parties to the agreement. Of course, contracts vary but there are a number of standard clauses that you must understand and certain things to look out for. There will be a general clause stating that the franchisor operates through franchised outlets, stating trademarks and the existence of an operating manual. This will be followed by a *grant* of the franchise and the time period for which the franchise is to operate.

Time period renewal
Make sure the franchise runs for a reasonable period – usually five to

ten years. This plays an important part in ensuring that you get your start-up costs back. Make sure the franchise is renewable after your period is up. Your *renewable option* should be present without any further payment; it should be renewable for a similar period to the original term and terms should be similar and not less favourable than you originally enjoyed. You need to protect yourself against unfair and unreasonable refusal to renew on the part of the franchisor.

As mentioned previously, there has been a case where a franchisor insisted on the property being revamped before renewal and then still refused to renew after considerable monies had been spent on doing just that. Don't always believe anything the franchisor says. It is essential that everything is obtained in writing and that the franchisor cannot unreasonably withhold consent to renew. GET IT ALL IN WRITING FROM DAY ONE!!!

Territory

Normally, you will be given an *exclusive territory* in which to operate the business. It is best to have details of this on an *actual* map. Find out where your neighbouring unit is, because obviously they will be competition for you. Make sure the franchisor cannot reduce your territory and find out on what basis he has allocated the territory, i.e. what market research has he carried out? Make your own inquiries about this, verify everything the franchisor says and get it stated in the contract. Be very cautious if a franchisor doesn't give you an exclusive territory or sufficient details.

As far as a franchisee is concerned it is in your interest to obtain the largest territory possible. However, this is not always ideal for the franchisor who will naturally be concerned that you may not exploit the full market potential. Some established franchisors have great market power and indeed refuse to grant territorial exclusivity. Such franchises should be considered with great care,but bear in mind that some excellent franchisors refuse to give territory on the ground that they need to be able to respond flexibly to market demand. This of course is to everyone's advantage.

A franchisor will be concerned that you may not work hard enough to make your business a success. He will expect you to achieve a certain level of performance failing which he may take back part of the territory or remove the exclusivity from the territory. Again this would not be a satisfactory arrangement for a franchisee since other factors, e.g. insufficient franchisor support, may be responsible for the low performance of the franchise.

Property

There will be various clauses in relation to your business property.

First ownership: it is better to lease the premises yourself. At least that way the increase in property value will benefit you or if the franchise agreement is terminated for any reason you will be able to continue another business on the same premises. However, a number of franchisors insist on leasing the premises themselves. They will then sublease and rent the premises to you, obviously at a markup. It can be an advantage that you don't have to lay out a premium but you need to know exactly what the terms are to be. Enquire whether some form of scheme is operated whereby you will share in the increase in property prices.

The franchisor will assist you in finding suitable sites. This service is usually included in the initial franchise fee. *Know* what your business requires. Do you need a high street position or will a good secondary position suffice? There will be a big price difference between the two. Do not overspend. Consider only what is within your financial limits.

There will be clauses stating that erection or conversion of the property must be at your expense and in accordance with the franchisor's plans and specifications and that you must complete works by a certain date. Make sure everything is priced carefully. Some franchisor's estimates on job costs are painfully unrealistic and outdated and franchisees find themselves in the position where costs have overrun to twice as much; they have premises they don't know what to do with and they can't raise extra funds to complete the works. Make sure that if this happens the franchisor is prepared to alter specifications to within the budget and the figures they originally provided.

The manual

You will have to undertake to comply with the operating manual which contains the know-how of the business. As the information in it is confidential a franchisor may refuse to allow you to see it before signing the contract. Insist on seeing a specimen and make sure that you will be able to comply with it. No reasonable or reputable franchisor can expect anyone to agree blindly to comply with something they have never seen. The information contained in the manual, together with the training, should impart the know-how and expertise to make your franchise unit a success. It should clearly illustrate how the business should be conducted. The franchise contract will contain clauses to restrict you from divulging the confidential information in the manual.

Advertising

In relation to advertising it is essential for you to verify:
1) How money for advertising is to be utilized?
2) What percentage of your royalty fee will go towards advertising?

3) Does it get paid into a separate fund?
4) How can you check that the money is being correctly spent, e.g.
   for advertising the franchise as opposed to merely advertising the
   franchise opportunity to get more franchisees?

Where independent advertising is allowed, the franchisor's approval
will usually be necessary – make sure it cannot be withheld unreasonably. A franchise chain should have a uniform image and therefore
franchisees will be restricted from unauthorized advertising – both
national or local. The franchisor will either undertake to spend a
certain amount of the royalty on advertising on behalf of the
franchisees or may set up a separate advertising fund to which every
franchisee contributes an equal amount, e.g. 10 per cent of their gross
income each week or month.

A franchisor may refine the system further by allowing a particular
franchisee to pay extra for additional advertising should they require
it. The franchisor will recommend how much advertising should be
carried out. Of course this will be more in the first year when the
business is unknown and will decrease with the build-up of goodwill.

Training
Training is an essential part of your franchise. You need to find out
what the training involves, where it takes place, who pays for it. Does it
cover training of staff? Will it be continued throughout your franchise
when necessary and will that cost extra? All this must be covered in the
contract.

Training and the operations manual
The franchisee should confirm:
* the minimum period of training
* the place of training
* any additional cost, e.g. travel and subsistance
* what the training will consist of, and who provides it

It is crucial that a franchisee is trained to the highest standards in
accordance with the expertise that the franchisor is offering. The
franchisor should impart all the skills necessary for that particular
franchise including staff selection, management and accounting procedures. The franchisor will be present when problems arise but the
franchisee can only make the business a success if he also becomes an
expert in the market.

Training should continue during the running of the franchise as no
doubt the market will change, new systems developed and products
improved. The franchisee should ensure that the franchisor will
continue to provide necessary training.

Stock and supplies
One of the most important aspects of your contract will be the clauses

dealing with *stock*, *supplies* and *equipment*. You need to verify mark-ups that the franchisor makes to you the franchisee. You need to know whether there is quality control on stock and goods supplied, how this is achieved and what happens if you are not happy with the quality – what will you be able to do about it? You must know how efficient supplies will be. What happens if there are delays? Will you be able to use alternative supplies? If not, will the franchisor compensate you for loss of sales due to insufficient stock? Do you have a choice of suppliers other than the franchisor? Some franchisors do allow you to purchase stock from other sources provided they approve. Make sure they cannot withhold approval unreasonably.

Exclusive supply

Some franchisors will be primarily concerned in distributing a particular product to you. You will be expected to purchase the product exclusively from the franchisor. The contract should state what will happen if the franchisor fails to provide the product. Under such conditions it should allow you to replenish from elsewhere.

Trading hours

In relation to your minimum opening hours be careful. Some franchisors very unrealistically base the profit projections *on all the hours God sends*. Convenience food stores are particularly notorious for this. You might face the problem, and it has happened, where you will be prosecuted for Sunday trading and realize that your profits are nowhere near the franchisor's projections. Make sure your contract states what trading hours are necessary to achieve your projections.

Price

A maximum/minimum price policy will normally be imposed. Make sure it gives you an adequate profit margin and that the goods are priced competitively with similar goods available in your area.

Royalty payments

Where **royalty payments** are due be cautious. If there is a low royalty fee it could mean that back-up services are poor, and if combined with a high initial fee it could mean that the franchisor will take your money and run. On the other hand, where the royalty fee is very high and because it is usually based on sales, you might find yourself in the unfortunate position of being pushed by the franchisor to increase sales at the cost of profitability. Always remember **turnover is vanity, profit is sanity**.

Nearly all franchisors rely on regular income from providing continuing services to the franchisee and obtaining a royalty payment on a weekly or monthly basis. This is usually calculated as a percentage of the gross income of the franchise unit. Sometimes a franchisor splits up the payments, e.g.

8 per cent royalty fee
1 per cent freight charge
1 per cent advertising fund
—

Total: 10 per cent

Don't be fooled by what he calls the payments. At the end of the day it is like paying a royalty of 10 per cent of the business's sales.

There is no royalty usually where the franchisor provides the franchisee with an exclusive product. In such cases the franchisor derives his income from a mark-up on the sale of the products to you. A test of reasonableness should be applied as to whether the royalty fee/mark-up is sensible depending on the services the franchisor provides. Royalty fees are seldom more than 10 per cent and mark-ups should be in accordance with the standard mark-ups for that type of business operation. Mark-ups on products and royalty fees need to be balanced and you should obtain an accountant's advice.

Sale or assignment by the franchisee

You need to have freedom and control in relation to selling or assigning your franchise at its market value. If you can only sell the business back to the franchisor, or the franchisor is unreasonable about sale to a third party, the value of business will suffer and you won't reap the benefits of your hard work.

You will usually have to give the franchisor first refusal and the franchisor's approval will be necessary for transfer to a third party. You must make sure he cannot withhold consent unreasonably, that an excessive transfer fee is not payable and that the franchisor cannot change the contract for the third party.

A franchisee may well wish to sell the franchised business for many reasons. In which case, he should consider the following:
*   If the franchisor inserts a clause stating they have a first option should the franchisee wish to sell, the franchisee should ensure that the valuation is based on an open market value of the franchise.
*   A franchisor will wish to control who the franchisee sells to. This is quite natural as an image needs to be preserved. However, the criteria by which a prospective purchaser will be judged by the franchisor should be clearly stated in the contract so that consent cannot be unreasonably withheld.

Sale or assignment by the franchisor

Most franchise contracts allow the franchisor to sell or assign the franchise without prior consultation or approval with franchisees. This unilateral aspect of the franchise relationship is very undesirable and should not be tolerated by any franchisee. As previously stated, there have been cases where a franchisor has assigned the franchise contract to a new franchisor who cannot provide the support and services the franchisees contracted for. In certain cases this has been so detrimental to the franchisees' business that it has then failed. You should endeavour to have a clause in the contract by which the franchisor can only sell/assign by a majority vote of the franchisees.

Termination of the contract

It is very important that you know the reasons for which the franchisor could terminate the agreement. The obvious reason is that you fail to comply with the contract. You need to ensure that the franchisor gives you a reasonable time period to rectify any breach. Some franchisors will list breaches which they think are so serious that they merit termination without notice, for instance, failure to report sales or selling non-franchise goods. Make sure anything listed is indeed a material breach and not something trivial.

Don't sign anything which allows the franchisor to terminate if, for example, you don't purchase a minimum quantity of goods or services, or you don't reach a certain sales quota. You do not know how your business will perform so don't commit yourself.

Standard clauses

All contracts will contain certain standard clauses which are to be expected because of the franchise relationship but you must make sure they are still reasonable. For example, a *secrecy clause* to protect knowhow; an *inspection clause* to make sure that the franchisor can enter the business premises at a reasonable time to ensure you are complying with the contract. An *indemnity clause* will state that you must indemnify the franchisor against loss, damage, liability by you or your agent. This is fine, provided it only applies if the franchisor is blameless. A *restraint of trade clause* will be present to prevent franchisees from engaging directly or indirectly in a business venture in competition with or in conflict with the franchisor in the territory for a given period of time – usually one year. It will probably also include a clause restraining employment of former employees in the franchise or of the franchisor.

A *choice of law clause* can be very important. It is particularly crucial where the franchisor is based abroad. Such a clause will state which law will govern the contract. For example, if the franchisor is based in France, will it be French or English law? Where the reader is thinking of taking up a 'foreign' franchise he needs to be particularly careful. Is the law that is stated as applying the most beneficial for him? If the franchisor is based say in the USA, the contract may still state that English law is to apply. However, this will not be wholly beneficial to the franchisee because the USA has franchise legislation while we don't and if the worst came to the worst the damages that could be obtained in a legal action in the USA would be greater than in England. Sometimes foreign franchisors specifically state that English law is to apply because they can get away with doing things here that legislation in their own countries makes illegal. Really, you should be able to choose which law is to govern the contract where the franchisor is based abroad.

An *arbitration clause* may also be present. This states that an 'arbitrator' (someone both the franchisor and franchisee agree upon) will decide any dispute. It has the advantage for the franchisor that the proceedings are private but there is no real advantage for the franchisee who may be stuck with an unsatisfactory decision. For the franchisee it is more beneficial to be able to resort to the usual legal remedies.

It is important to remember that whether or not such a clause exists a franchisee can approach the BFA under its arbitration scheme (see Chapter 4). The advantage of their scheme, as discussed earlier, is that franchisees only pay one third of the costs even if they lose and pay nothing if they win. Only the franchisee can initially elect to use the scheme. The only problem is that the franchisor can refuse to refer the dispute to arbitration. Then the franchisee has no choice but to go to court.

In case of *death or incapacity* you need to ensure that provisions are made by which the franchisor must assist to continue the business until it can be sold profitably, or that the franchisor buys the business at market value or helps the franchisee's dependants take over. It is vital that you take out *life assurance*. Both the bank and your franchisor will usually insist on this anyway.

A franchisor may try to put a *decisions in writing* clause in the contract stating that the franchisor is only to be bound by statements/ promises made in writing. You should not accept such a clause. All franchisors make oral representations to induce a franchisee to enter into the contract. Don't trust a franchisor who is not prepared to be bound by oral representations. Let him put his money where his mouth is. If anything, you should ensure that oral representations which induce you to sign the contract are included and a part of the overall agreement, for example as an appendix to the agreement.

Some franchisors may have the nerve to try to go even further and put a clause in the contract stating the contract is the entire agreement and that you have not relied on other oral or written representations. Obviously you have relied on information and representations by the franchisor so don't accept such a clause.

In order to protect yourself further request a '*no discrimination between franchisees*' clause. A reputable and fair minded franchisor should not object. There have been cases where some franchisees were given preferential discounts and company-owned shops supplied with superior stock to that of its franchisees.

In other countries, for example, the USA, Franchisee Associations are very popular and provide an invaluable function. You should have a clause in the contract allowing you to set up such an organization. Be very wary of a franchisor who will not agree to it. The chances are he will be pursuing a divide and rule policy between the franchisees and this will certainly not benefit you.

Annual meeting and franchisee association
It is extremely important that franchisees be able to meet at least once a year to discuss important issues and exchange ideas. A clause should be inserted to require the franchisor to arrange such events. It should be stated who is to bear the cost. Normally the franchisor will arrange the event with franchisees contributing to the cost. A franchisee association is extremely useful. Some people fear that it may be like a trade union. This is unlikely. It is useful for both franchisees and franchisors. For instance, if a particular franchisee is letting standards slip other franchisees within the group will soon put him right as they will not want their image tarnished. On the other hand, if for example the franchisor is not providing sufficient support, the franchisees will have more impact if they act together in approaching the franchisor with their complaints.

Depending on the nature of the franchised business there may be other clauses in the contract, and you should be aware of their implications. I will discuss some of these now.

Insurance
The franchisee will have to effect his own insurance. The franchisor will do likewise. You would be well advised to ask for the franchisor's assistance in negotiating suitable policies with an insurance company for the franchise chain. This will reduce costs. The franchisee should carry personal insurance in case of incapacity. In most cases the bank will insist on this.

Minimum wage provision
The franchisee is in control of hiring and firing employees. It is rare that wage disputes arise but there is always the possibility that a franchisee may get involved, and of course this would reflect badly on the whole chain. Thus it is not unreasonable for the franchisor to impose a minimum wage policy in the contract to avoid any problems.

Vehicles used in the franchised business
For those franchises which require specially equipped vehicles the contract will contain provisions regarding ownership of those vehicles. The franchisee may have already paid for them in the initial fee or may

lease or hire them. It would be in the franchisee's interests to have a clause outlining the rate at which the vehicles should depreciate and an agreement under which the franchisor will buy back the vehicles should the franchise agreement terminate.

Liability of the franchisor to his franchisee
No doubt some franchisors will want to exempt liability in contract or in tort. In such cases the Unfair Contract Terms Act 1977 must be considered. It is not entirely clear how this Act applies to franchise agreements. Sections two and three of this Act regulate the exclusion of liability or negligence or breach of contract. As far as you are concerned liability for death or personal injury **cannot** be excluded and other exemptions have to satisfy the test of reasonableness.

Franchisor third party liability for defaults of franchisee
There is a real risk that the franchisor could be held liable to third parties if a franchisee goes bankrupt or into liquidation. Therefore the franchisor will wish to protect himself. It will not be unusual therefore for him to require the franchisee to declare the franchisee relationship on the premises, on order forms and on other stationery. This will be especially important in relation to trade creditors. Normally amounts owing to customers will be insignificant.

The franchisor usually sets up an arrangement whereby they grant a master licence to a subsidiary which in turn franchises to the franchisee. The franchisee pays the franchise fee to the subsidiary who then pays it to the holding company:

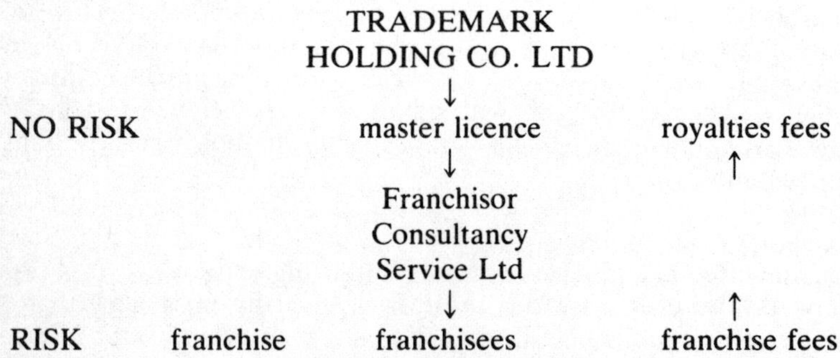

The theory of doing it this way is that licence of a trademark is unlikely to result in liability to third parties. Thus, there is only a risk for the subsidiary.

The situation may be varied so that the Holding Co. Ltd grants the franchisee the licence, use of intellectual property and manages the advertising, while the subsidiary enters into the franchise agreements and exercises control. The real reason for doing it this way is **tax**. The problem of third party liability is a bonus. Usually franchisors adopt simpler structures – but it really depends on the amount of money at stake. Either way, you will probably find that the franchisor has arranged his business in such a way as to avoid liabilities to third parties.

Severance clause
This will state that if any part of the contract is held invalid or unenforceable it will not affect the validity or enforceability of the remainder.

You will need to research and understand every clause of the contract. Do not, as discussed earlier, go to just any solicitor; go to a commercial solicitor who understands franchising. Don't be afraid to ask for amendments or additions or deletions to the contract. If the franchisor is not reasonable you should not continue. If the franchisor is honest and reputable he should welcome your comments and be prepared to make the contract equitable for all franchisees, if it isn't already. Treat the whole research process like a game of chess. You must be practical, methodical and unemotional. No matter how fantastic the franchise opportunity seems to be the contract should represent a real picture of what has been agreed and should be equitable.

Always remember you cannot ask enough questions. There is no greater force in business than facts combined with ideas. Once armed with all the facts look at them as they are. Use them to your advantage. List all the pros and cons on a piece of paper. Think about it for a few weeks and ask your solicitor's and accountant's advice.

Remember also what the outcome of research can be. You could analyse a glass of water into its chemical components and be left with nothing to drink and, as Thomas Huxley said, 'there is no sadder sight in the world than to see a beautiful theory killed by a brutal fact'. If this happens with your franchise, and you realize that the franchise is not as marvellous as the franchisor claims at least you will not have invested your money on a bad business opportunity.

On the other hand, your research could have positive results and you will be able to proceed with confidence. However, always remember there is no such thing as 'zero risk'.

There follows a specimen short form contract which you should look through to familiarize yourself with what a contract looks like, plus a specimen Wimpy contract which should also be of interest to you.

Franchise agreement – short form

By John Adams and K. V. Prichard Jones

REPRINTED FROM FRANCHISING: PRACTICE AND PRECEDENTS IN BUSINESS FORMAT FRANCHISING BY KIND PERMISSION OF THE PUBLISHERS, BUTTERWORTHS

Dated .... 19........

1 Parties
.... whose [registered office *or* principal place of business] is at (*address*) ('the Franchisor') (1)
.... whose [registered office *or* principal place of business] is at (*address*) ('the Franchisee') (2)

2 Definitions
The following terms shall have the following meanings:
2.1 'Advertising Contribution': ....% of Gross Turnover (as defined in clause [3.12] of the Conditions] of the Business
2.2 'Business': the use (for mutual benefit) of the Mark and the Know-How in the business of trading under the Permitted Name in the style and manner stipulated by the Franchisor for (*insert details of Business to be carried out*)
2.3 'Conditions': the Standard Conditions and Special Conditions (if any) annexed to this Agreement which shall be deemed to be incorporated in this Agreement in their entirety
2.4 'Continuing Fees': the franchise fees of ....% of Gross Turnover (as defined in clause [3.12] of the Conditions) of the Business
2.5 'Financial Year': each year during the Term ending on the .... (*year end date*)
2.6 'Initial Fee': the initial franchise fee of £.......... (........pounds)
2.7 'Know-How': the operational systems and methods of the Franchisor as divulged to the Franchisee from time to time during the Term
2.8 'Location': the premises shortly described as .... or such other premises as are approved by the Franchisor during the Term
2.9 'Manual': the confidential written systems of and regulations for the operation of the Business issued and amended by the Franchisor from time to time during the Term incorporating part of the Know-How and deemed to form part of this Agreement (Serial Number ....)
2.10 'Mark': the [Legend] [and design] and the logos associated with the same and any additional or substitute Marks which the Franchisor shall deem suitable for the Business during the Term

2.11 'Minimum Package':
    2.11:1 The equipment products literature stock of all types and
    2.11:2 The minimum staff levels [at the location] stipulated in the
         manual from time to time during the Term
2.12 'Payment Dates':
    2.12:1 For the Initial Fee: on the signing of this Agreement
    2.12:2 For the Advertising Contributions and the Continuing Fees: the
         [tenth] day of each [calendar month] during the Term in respect
         of the Business during the immediately preceding calendar
         month
2.13 'Permitted Name': the permitted business name of the Franchisee
which shall be '........'
2.14 'Term': .... years from .... 19....... (the Commencement Date)
and expiring on .... 19....... (the Expiry Date) unless sooner determined
as provided in the Conditions
2.15 'Territory': the geographical area of (*insert description of area*) [and
shown edged red on the map annexed to this Agreement]

3 The Right

In consideration of the payment of the Initial Fee the Insurance Premium the
Advertising Contribution and the Continuing Fees by the Franchisee to the
Franchisor and of and subject to the agreements on the part of the Franchisee
in this Agreement the Franchisor grants to the Franchisee the right of using
the Mark and the Know-How only:

3.1 In the Business

3.2 At and from the Location

3.3 Within the Territory

3.4 For the Term

3.5 Under the Permitted Name

3.6 In accordance with the Manual

Dated ....day of .... 19........

Signed by .... (*name of director*) for and on behalf of .... (*name of
Franchisor*)

Signed by .... (*name of director*) for and on behalf of .... (*name of
Franchisee*)

STANDARD CONDITIONS

1 Title

The Franchisor warrants that it is the beneficial owner of the Mark and Know-
How

2 Franchisor's obligations

The Franchisor agrees as follows:

2.1 Training

To provide within 90 days of this date at a place chosen by the Franchisor training in the conduct of the Business for one director of the Franchisee and all the initial employees of the Franchisee the cost of which is included in the Initial Fee

2.2 Manual

To issue the Franchisee with the Manual and to update it (provided the same shall remain the property of the Franchisor)

2.3 Advertising

To undertake an advertising and promotional programme for the Mark in selected areas of the British Isles in such manner as it considers appropriate using the Advertising Contribution

2.4 Advertising bank account

To pay the Advertising Contribution (together with similar contributions from [stores *or* outlets] owned by the Franchisor) into a separate bank account of the Franchisor maintained for that purpose only

2.5 Expenses

To issue to the Franchisee an account of the total expenditure by the Franchisor on advertising and promotion in each Financial Year of the term provided that the Franchisor shall be entitled to recoup at any time from the total of the Advertising Contribution from all its franchisees in any year any excess of such expenditure over the total of receipts of the Advertising Contributions in previous or future years

2.6 Exclusive

Not to undertake on its own behalf nor to grant any franchise to any other person or entity in respect of the Business in the Territory (subject as appears later in these Conditions)

2.7 Information

Throughout the Term to consider and respond to all reasonable requests from the Franchisee for information and assistance concerning the Business

2.8 Supply Conditions

To procure that products for the Business shall be supplied to the Franchisee by the Franchisor or its approved suppliers on the same terms as those supplies to [stores *or* outlets] operated by the Franchisor itself in the United Kingdom

[2.9 Additional sales

To permit the Franchisee to sell such equipment and similar items in addition to the Minimum Package in order to satisfy specific orders or demand subject to the prior approval by the Franchisor of such equipment and other items]

3 Franchisee's obligations

The Franchisee agrees throughout the Term:

3.1 Training first

    3.1:1   Not to commence the Business until [one director of] the Franchisee and all its senior employees have received training from and have been approved as competent by the Franchisor

3.1:2   To notify the Franchisor whenever it employs new staff in the Business

3.1:3   Not to permit any person to be employed in the Business unless such person is first trained and approved as competent by the Franchisor

3.1:4   To procure that all its executives and employees attend further training during the Term when required by the Franchisor

3.2 Registered user

Where necessary to become the registered user of the Mark or to execute on demand from the Franchisor such formal licence for records purposes as may be required in the United Kingdom

3.3 Authority

To display at the Location and on all stationery and any literature used by the Franchisee the text stipulated in the Manual from time to time disclosing that the Franchisee is licensed by the Franchisor and is not a branch or agent of the Franchisor

3.4 Mark

3.4:1   Constantly to protect and promote the goodwill attached to the Mark (which the Franchisee acknowledges is of great value)

3.4:2   To hold any additional goodwill generated by the Franchisee for the Mark or the Permitted Name as bare trustee for the Franchisor

3.4:3   Not to cause or permit any damage to the Mark or the title of the Franchisor to it or assist others to do so

3.4:4   Not to use the Mark the Know-How or the Permitted Name except directly in the Business

3.4:5   Not to use the Mark the Know-How or the Permitted Name in any manner after the Term or other sooner determination of the Agreement

3.4:6   Not to use the Mark or any derivation of the same in the corporate name (if any) of the Franchisee

3.5 Secrecy

Not at any time during or after the Term:

3.5:1   to divulge to any third party any information concerning the Business the Franchisor the Know-How or any other systems or methods of the Franchisor used in the Business (especially that contained in the Manual)

3.5:2   to copy in any way in any part of the Manual

3.6 Disclosure

Not to employ any person in the Business until that person has signed a non-disclosure undertaking in the form approved by the Franchisor from time to time

3.7 Volume

To use its best endeavours to achieve the greatest volume of business for the Business at the Location consistent with good service to the public

3.8 No other business

Not without the prior approval of the Franchisor:

    3.8:1   to permit any other business venture to operate or trade at or from the Location

    3.8:2   to extend the scope or range of the Business at the Location

    3.8:3   to engage directly or indirectly in any other business other than the Business

3.9 No illegal use

Not to engage in any activities in the Business which may be contrary to law or governments or other regulations

3.10 Payments

To pay the Initial Fee the Continuing Fees and the Advertising Contribution (without demand deduction or set-off) to the Franchisor (or as it directs) on each of the Payment Dates (time being of the essence)

3.11 VAT contingency

Whenever applicable to pay to the Franchisor VAT or any other tax or duty replacing the same during the Term charged or calculated on the amount of the Initial Fee the Continuing Fees and the Advertising Contribution

3.12 Calculations

To calculate the Continuing Fees and the Advertising Contribution on the gross turnover of the Business arising directly or indirectly from the conduct of the Business in the Territory during each calendar week of the Term (and for any period less than a complete calendar week) and gross turnover shall include

    3.12:1   all credit sales of whatever nature whether or not the Franchisee has received payment of the outstanding accounts by the Payment Date relevant to the week when such credit sales were made

    3.12:2   all cash sales of whatever nature made but not invoiced by the Franchisee in each week

    3.12:3   all services performed and business dealings whatsoever (other than purchases) made or conducted in the Territory by the Business during each week

But shall exclude

    3.12:4   any VAT

    3.12:5   any customer refunds or credits arising from the supply of defective goods or services or the like provided that such refunds or credits shall only be deducted from gross turnover in the calendar week in which they are paid or allowed to the customer

3.13 Service report

On each Monday of each week to post by first-class mail (or by electronic means if required by the Franchisor) to the Franchisor complete and accurate statements in the form approved by the Franchisor in the Manual) of the sales and services performed by the Business since the last such Payment Date

3.14 Accurate accounts

To keep accurate books and accounts in respect of the Business in accordance with good accountancy custom in the United Kingdom and the standards set out in the Manual and to:

    3.14:1 Accountants

           have them audited at the expense of Franchisee once a year during the Term by the firm of Chartered Accountants nominated by the Franchisor

    3.14:2 Audit

           submit the whole of such audited accounts to the Franchisor within three months of the end of such year

    3.14:3 Custody

           keep them for not less than [3] years

    3.14:4 Inspection

           permit the Franchisor to inspect and take copies (at the expense of the Franchisor) of any financial information or records it requires (on reasonable prior notice in the event of inspection after normal business hours)

    3.14:5 Financial Year

           procure that each financial year or period of the Business shall be the same as the Financial Year

3.15 Discrepancies

In the event of discrepancies (amounting in total to more than [2%] per year of gross sales) in any such books or accounts to permit accountants nominated by the Franchisor but at the expense of the Franchisee to undertake audits of the same in each year of the Term of the Franchisor (at intervals at the discretion of the Franchisor) on reasonable notice and during normal business hours

3.16 VAT report

Within 14 days of submission or receipt to supply to the Franchisor a copy of each VAT return and/or assessment in respect of the Business

3.17 Conduct of the Business

Not to conduct the Business except:

    3.17:1 Standards

           In respect of services to the standards and quality and in the standard style and by the methods stipulated in the Manual from time to time

    3.17:2 Regulations

           In confirmity with all relevant government or other regulations

    3.17:3 Financial systems

           Under proper and comprehensive financial systems and controls as approved or stipulated by the Franchisor

    3.17:4 Venue

           At or from the Location or such other venue first approved by the Franchisor

3.17:5 Inside Territory
Inside the Territory

[3.17:6 Equipment
With the equipment part of the Minimum Package in good and reliable condition]

[3.17:7 Staff
With the staff part of the minimum package at full complement and fully trained and approved by the Franchisor]

3.17:8 Dealerships
In accordance with the rules and regulations of any dealership or distributorship arrangements for any of the equipment or products dealt in by the Business

3.18 Insurance policy

3.18:1 To maintain and pay all premiums in respect of a comprehensive insurance policy (in terms approved by the Franchisor) issued by an insurer nominated by the Franchisor in respect of the Location for all items stored there and for the business

3.18:2 To note on such policy that:

3.18:2.1 the Franchisor shall be covered by such policy in respect of all claims arising from activities at the Location or in the Business or of the Franchisee which are risks covered by such policy

3.18:2.2 the insurer shall notify the Franchisor in the event of any late premium payment by the Franchisee

3.19 Inspection of Premises

To permit the Franchisor or its representatives to inspect the Location at any time during the Term

3.20 Right notices

To affix such patent copyright or trade mark ownership notices to any stationery or literature used by the Franchisee in the Business as the Franchisor may require from time to time

3.21 Infringement indemnity

To indemnify the Franchisor from:

3.21:1 any alleged unauthorised use or infringement of any patent trade mark copyright or other intellectual property (other than the Mark and Know-How) by the Franchisee

3.21:2 any claim by any third party in respect of the conduct of the Business or the conduct or neglect of the Franchisee

3.21:3 any infringement by the Franchisee of any relevant regulations

3.22 Infringement notice

To notify the Franchisor of any suspected infringement of the intellectual property or other rights of the Franchisor and to take such reasonable action thereupon as the Franchisor directs at the expense of the Franchisor

3.23 Payment

Not to purchase any supplies [courses] products equipment or literature for the Business except from the Franchisor or (with the consent of the Franchisor) its approved suppliers to ensure even standards of quality of products and services from all the franchisees of the Franchisor and:

    3.23:1 to pay the Franchisor for any equipment stationery or other items so purchased within 21 days of dispatch by the Franchisor

    3.23:2 to pay promptly any other suppliers of the Franchisee in accordance with their usual terms and conditions

3.24 No sub-franchise

Not to grant any sub-franchise in respect of the Mark the Know-How or the Business

3.25 Promotions

    3.25:1 To advertise the Business in the Territory in accordance with the requirements of the Franchisor set out in the Manual from time to time

    3.25:2 (As part of such obligation) to expend not less than ......% of the gross turnover of the Business in each Financial Year upon local advertising and promotional activities

    3.25:3 To participate in such promotional activities for the Business in the Territory as the Franchisor requires during the Term

3.26 Assignment

Not to assign transfer or otherwise deal with the Right or this Agreement or the Business in any way without the prior approval of the Franchisor which shall not be unreasonably withheld in the following circumstances:

    3.26:1 if the proposed assignee is acceptable to the Franchisor and shall agree to be bound by the terms and conditions of the standard franchise agreement used by the Franchisor at the time of such proposed assignment for the residue of the Term and

    3.26:2 if the Franchisee shall pay to the Franchisor the reasonable costs and expenses incurred by the Franchisor in the assessment of each proposed assignee

3.27 Director reliance

(As the Right has been granted to the Franchisee by the Franchisor in reliance upon the quality of the directors and shareholders of the Franchisee) not to permit any change in the same without the prior approval of the Franchisor which shall not be unreasonably withheld subject to the provisions in sub-clauses [3.26:1 and 3.26:2) of these conditions

3.28 Prices

    3.28:1 Not to charge any customer any prices in excess of those stipulated in the Manual from time to time

    3.28:2 Not to sell any items or provide any services to any person or entity associated with the Franchisee or its shareholders except at prices usually charged by the Franchisee to its non-connected customers

3.29 No competition

And for a period of [two] years afterwards:

    3.29:1 Not to engage directly or indirectly in any capacity in any business venture competitive with or likely to damage the surviving goodwill of the Business in the Territory or in any territory any business venture competitive with any business of the other franchisee of the Franchisor

3.29:2 Not to solicit the customers or former customers of the Business with the intent of taking their custom

3.29:3 Not to employ any employee or former employees who were employed in the Business by the Franchisee or by the Franchisor or any other franchisee of the Franchisor

and to procure that all directors and shareholders of the Franchisee enter into direct covenants of similar content with the Franchisor

3.30 Grant back

To notify the Franchisor and provide full details of any improvements in the methods systems products or programmes described by the Franchisor in the Manual or employed in the Business and to permit the Franchisor to incorporate free of charge any such improvements in its Manual for the benefit of the Franchisor and all its franchisees.

[3.31 Premises

3.31:1 To maintain the Location in good decorative repair and condition

3.31:2 To alter the exterior and interior decoration signs and furnishings of the Location when required to do so by the Franchisor in accordance with any amendments it may make to the house style of the Business

3.31:3 To observe and perform all its obligations under any lease or tenancy of the Location]

4 Expiry procedure

On expiry or termination of this Agreement the Franchisee agrees:

4.1 Not to endeavour to surrender the telephones used in the Business nor to hinder the transfer of such telephones to such person as the Franchisor directs

4.2 To return to the Franchisor all stationery used in the Business

4.3 To return to the Franchisor all publicity promotional and advertising material

4.4 To return to the Franchisor the Manual in good condition and without having made any copy of the Manual

4.5 To sign such notification of cessation of use of the Mark as is necessary for recording at the Trade Marks Registry

4.6 To cease carrying on the Business immediately

4.7 (When the Franchisee is the tenant or lessee of the Franchisor at the Location) to surrender to the Franchisor the relevant tenancy agreement or lease immediately upon such expiry or termination and to vacate the Location immediately

5 Expiry financial procedure

The Franchisee agrees:

5.1 Four weeks prior to the expiry of the Term or three weeks after receipt of notice of termination of this Agreement to furnish to the Franchisor a complete and accurate up-to-date list of customers of the Business with estimates of turnover of the Business to such expiry or termination date and

5.2 Thereupon to pay the Continuing Fees and the Advertising Contribution on the estimated Gross Turnover to such date and

5.3 Not later than the first Friday after such date to pay to the Franchisor any additional amount of the Continuing Fees and the Advertising Contribution calculated on actual gross turnover of the Business to such date

6 Miscellaneous

It is further agreed between the parties:

6.1 Reservation of rights

6.1.1   All the rights not specifically and expressly granted to the Franchisee in this Agreement are reserved to the Franchisor

6.1:2   The Franchisor may grant a licence to any entity to manufacture any products in the Territory or elsewhere for use in connection with the Business or displaying the Mark or for other purposes (except in competition with the Franchisee in the Territory) without any liability to the Franchisee

6.2 Interest

Without prejudice to the rights of the Franchisor and the condition that the Initial Fee the Advertising Contribution and the Continuing Fees are paid on time (time being of the essence) all sums due to the Franchisor which are not paid on the due date shall bear interest from day to day at the annual rate of ....% over the current Bank plc daily base interest rate with a minimum of ......%

6.3 Payment not on time

In the event that the Franchisee fails to pay any money due to the Franchisor on time the Franchisor may

6.3:1   cease immediately to take orders from and to deliver goods and services to the Franchisee

6.3:2   afterwards impose whatever credit limit it considers appropriate in respect of the Business of the Franchisee

6.4 Receipt

The receipt of money by the Franchisor shall not prevent either of the parties questioning the correctness of any statement in respect of that money

6.5 Force majeure

Both parties shall be released from their respective obligations in the event of national emergency war prohibitive governmental regulations or if any other cause beyond the control of the parties shall render performance of the Agreement impossible provided that this clause shall only have effect at the discretion of the Franchisor except when such event renders performance impossible for a continuous period of [12] calendar months

6.6 Severance

In the event that any provision of this agreement or these Conditions is declared by any judicial or other competent authority to be void voidable illegal or otherwise unenforceable [or indications of the same are received by either of the parties from any relevant competent authority] [the parties shall amend that provision in such reasonable manner as achieves the intention of the parties without illegality or the Franchisor may sever the offending provision from the same at its discretion *or* the remaining provisions of this Agreement shall remain in full force and effect unless the Franchisor in the Franchisor's discretion decides that the effect of such declaration is to defeat the original intention of the parties in which event the Franchisor shall be entitled to terminate this Agreement by [30] days' notice to the Franchisee and the provisions of clause [4] shall apply accordingly]

6.7 Low sales

The Franchisor may terminate this Agreement in the event that reasonably substantial turnover (which shall be calculated by the Franchisor on the basis of demographic and socio-economic data in respect of the Territory and the performance of its other franchisees) arising from the Business at the Location is not achieved within two years of the Commencement Date of the Agreement or for a continuous period of twelve months at any time afterwards during the Term provided that the Franchisor shall have the right (but not the duty):

6.7:1   then to appoint management personnel to supervise the Business at the expense of the Business to assist the Franchisor to increase sales and/or

6.7:2   to reduce the area of the Territory in proportion to such sales

6.8 New outlets

6.8:1   In the event that the Franchisor decides that the Territory is sufficiently large geographically and has a sufficiently large population to justify one or more further outlets for the Business in the Territory it may notify the Franchisee of such decision and on receipt of such notice the Franchisee shall have the right to open such further outlet elsewhere than at the Location in an area of the Territory nominated by the Franchisor) provided that the Franchisee informs the Franchisor within 90 days of such notice of its agreement to do so

6.8:2   In the event that the Franchisee fails to notify the Franchisor of such agreement within 90 days or fails to open such further outlet in the Territory within six months of such notice the Franchisor shall have the right to reduce the Territory to enable it to provide an exclusive area in which a new franchisee may trade using the Mark and the Know-How without liability to the Franchisee

6.9 Prior obligations

The expiration or termination of this Agreement shall not relieve either of the parties of their respective prior obligations or impair or prejudice their respective rights against the other

6.10 Discretion

No decision exercise of discretion judgement opinion or approval of any matter mentioned in this Agreement or arising from it shall be deemed to have been made by the Franchisor except if in writing and shall be at its sole discretion unless otherwise expressly provided in this Agreement or these Conditions

6.1 Notice

6.11:1 Any notice to be served on either of the parties by the other shall be sent by prepaid recorded delivery or registered post (as the case may be) or by telex or by electronic mail and shall be deemed to have been received by the addressee within 72 hours of posting or 24 hours if sent by telex or by electronic mail to the correct telex or electronic mail number of the addressee

6.11:2 Each of the parties shall notify the other of any change of address or number as soon as practicable and in any event within 48 hours of such change

6.12 No agency

The parties are not partners or joint venturers nor is the Franchisee able to act as the agent or to pledge the credit of the Franchisor in any way

6.13 Whole agreement

The Franchisee acknowledges that this Agreement and these Conditions contain the whole agreement between the parties and it had not relied upon any oral or written representations made to it by the Franchisor or its employees or agents and has made its own independent investigations into all matters relevant to the Business

6.14 Breach procedure

In the event that the Franchise fails to observe or perform any of its obligations under this Agreement or these Conditions in any way then the Franchisor may terminate this Agreement on 30 days' written notice and

6.14:1 notwithstanding such notice period if the breach complained of its incapable of remedy this Agreement shall terminate absolutely on service of such notice

6.14:2 in every other case if the breach complained of is remedied to the satisfaction of the Franchisor within the notice period this Agreement shall not terminate

6.14:3 no waiver of any breach of those obligations shall constitute a waiver of any further or continuing breach of the same

6.15 Insolvency

If the Franchisee enters into liquidation or suffers a receiver to be appointed to it or to any of its assets or makes a composition with any of its creditors (or the equivalent in Scotland) the Franchisor may at any time afterwards terminate this Agreement on notice with immediate effect and:

6.15:1 no creditor agent representative or trustee of the Franchisee shall have the right to use the Mark or the Know-How or continue the Business without the prior consent of the Franchisor

6.15:2 until payment of all money due to the Franchisor from the Franchisee on any account the Franchisor shall have a lien on any of the stock literature or other products held by the Franchisee

6.16 Assignment

The Franchisor may assign charge or otherwise deal with this Agreement in any way

6.17 Renewal option

The Franchisee shall have the option to extend the Term for a further period of .... years commencing on the day following the Expiry Date subject to the following:

6.17:1 service of notice of extension by the Franchisee on the Franchisor not later than ...... calendar months prior to the Expiry Date and

6.17:2 payment by the Franchisee to the Franchisor not later than two calendar months prior to the Expiry Date of a renewal fee of ......% of gross turnover of the Business during 12 calendar months prior to the first day of the calendar month in which such notice is served or the then current Initial Fee charged by the Franchisor to its franchisees (whichever is the less) and

6.17:3 proper performance and observance by the Franchisee of all its obligations under this Agreement throughout the Term and

6.17:4 execution by the Franchisee of a new franchise agreement in the standard form used by the Franchisor at the time of service of such notice in respect of the further period of .... years without any option to review

6.18 Further extension

In the event that any regulation requires the Franchisor to extend the Term beyond the period of a further .... years as mentioned in clause [6.17] of these Conditions then the same provisions and procedure as set out there shall apply to any such subsequent extension.

6.19 Death or incapacity

6.19:1 In the event of the death of an individual Franchisee the personal representatives of the Franchisee shall have six calendar months from the date of death to notify the franchisor of their decision

6.19:1.1 to continue the Business whereupon such personal representatives shall be deemed to be proposed assignees of the Business or

6.19:1.2 to assign the Business to any of the heirs of the Franchisee or to a third party

whereupon the provisions set out in subclauses [3.26:1 and 3.26:2] of these Conditions shall apply

6.19:2 In the event of the incapacity of [the Franchisee *or* .... (*the key director of the Franchise*)] at any time or after such death (but prior to any such decision by such personal representatives) the

Franchisor shall have the right (but not the duty) to appoint management personnel to supervise the conduct of the Business (at the expense of the Business) to ensure that the Business shall operate in a satisfactory manner to preserve the goodwill of the Mark pending the recovery of the Franchisee or such decision

6.19:3 If so requested by the Franchisee (or the personal representatives of the Franchisee) the Franchisor may act as a non-exclusive agent for the sale of the Business and in such event shall be paid its expenses and fees as follows:

6.19:3.1 in the event that the assigneee is found by the franchisee [3%] of the sale price of the Business (including any lease premium and fixtures and fittings) or

6.19:3.2 in the event that the assignee is found by the Franchisor [5%] of such sale price

6.20 Headings

Headings contained in these Conditions are for reference purposes only and shall not be incorporated in the Agreement or these Conditions and shall not be deemed to be any indication of the meaning of the clauses and sub-clauses to which they relate

6.21 Proper law

English law only shall apply to this Agreement in every particular (including formation) and the English Courts shall have sole jurisdiction to which the parties exclusively submit

---

WIMPY

Counter Service Franchise Agreement

Contents

This Agreement

made the   day of   19   between UNITED
BISCUITS (UK) LIMITED, whose Registered Office is at 12 Hope Street,
Edinburgh EH2 4DD ('the Franchisor') **OF THE ONE PART** operating through
its appointed agent, Wimpy International Limited, whose Registered Office is
at 214 Chiswick High Road, London W4 1PD
and ('the Franchisee') **OF THE OTHER PART**

Recitals

Whereas, the Franchisor is the registered proprietor of the Trade Marks:
969470, 969471, B720112, B720113, B720114, B815867, B902066 and
B1112308, (hereinafter called 'the Trade Marks') being Trade Marks which
the Franchisee wishes to use in connection with hamburgers prepared by the
Franchisee from patties and buns supplied by the Franchisor or by such other
suppliers as the Franchisor may from time to time appoint and prepared and
served by the Franchisee in accordance with the Manuals.

Whereas, the Franchisor is engaged in the business of franchising and
operating limited menu, fast food restaurants throughout the United Kingdom
and, in connection therewith, licensing the use of the Trade Marks, which said
restaurants are hereinafter referred to as Wimpy; and

Whereas, the Franchisor has established a high reputation as to the quality of
products and services available at Wimpy, which said high reputation and
goodwill has been and continues to be a unique benefit to the Franchisor and
its Franchisees; and

Whereas, the Franchisee recognises the benefits to be derived from being
identified with and licensed by the Franchisor, and being able to utilise the
Names and Trade Marks which the Franchisor makes available to its
Franchisees; and

Whereas, the Franchisee desires to be franchised to use the Trade Marks in
connection with the sale of Menu items, as specified by the Franchisor from
time to time.

Now therefore it is hereby agreed between the Parties as follows:–

1. Franchise Payment:
Services by the Franchisor

A. Franchise Payment

The Franchisor acknowledges payment to it by the Franchisee of the total sum
of £   plus VAT consisting of £   plus VAT, already paid
by way of deposit as and for a franchise fee, and £   plus VAT for
initial assistance essential to the Franchisee consisting of the training and the
services detailed in Paragraph B below. The Franchisee acknowledges that
the grant of the franchise constitutes the sole consideration for the payment of
the franchise fee and that the said sum shall be fully earned by the Franchisor
upon execution and delivery hereof. No further franchise fee shall by payable
during the term hereof.

B. Services by the Franchisor

The Franchisor agrees during the term of this Franchise Agreement to use its best efforts to maintain the high reputation of Wimpy and in connection therewith to make available to the Franchisee:

1. The Specifications and plans for the shop-fitting of the building, equipment, furnishings, decor, layout, and signs identified with Wimpy, together with advice and consultation concerning them but excluding any charges incurred as a result of consultation of and services provided by external professional specialists such as (but without prejudice to the generality of the foregoing) Structural Engineers, Quantity Surveyors, Architects, the charges for whom will be paid for by the Franchisee whether such charges were incurred by the Franchisor or the Franchisee.

2. A pre-opening training programme conducted at the Franchisor's training school and at a Wimpy.

3. Opening supervision and assistance from employees of the Franchisor at the Franchisee's premises.

4. Opening promotion programmes conducted under the direction of the Franchisor's marketing department.

5. The Franchisor's confidential Procedural Manuals current from time to time, (hereinafter collectively called 'the Manuals') shall form an integral part of this Agreement. Copies of the Manuals are (or will be) delivered and loaned to the Franchisee for the term hereof and shall be returned to the Franchisor at the cost of the Franchisee upon termination of this Agreement for whatsoever cause and the Franchisee agrees not to make any copies of the Manuals. The Franchisor's confidential current Design and Technical manual will not be delivered and loaned to the Franchisee but will be available for inspection by the Franchisee, his employees and agents upon request to the Franchisor.

6. Such merchandising, marketing and advertising support, advice, and such research data as may be from time to time developed by the Franchisor and deemed by it to be helpful in the operation of Wimpy.

7. The buying power, product quality assurance, and distribution expertise of the Franchisor.

8. Consultation and advice by the Franchisor's Operations Executives on a regular basis.

9. Such special techniques, food preparation instructions, new restaurant services and other operational developments as may be from time to time developed by the Franchisor and deemed by it to be helpful in the operation of Wimpy.

2. Franchise Grant:
Similar Business: Term
A. Franchise Grant

1. The Franchisor grants to the Franchisee the right subject to due acceptance by the Registrar of Trade Marks of the application agreed to be made under clause 10(A)(4) hereof to the use by the Franchisee of the Trade Marks in relation to hamburgers provided always that such right should be limited to hamburgers which are prepared and sold at the Premises in accordance with the terms and conditions of this Agreement.

2. The Franchisor grants to the Franchisee the right subject to the agreement of the Franchisor to the use of the copyright of the Franchisor in any printed matter, distinctive features, menus, decor, fabric and any other matter pertaining to this Agreement.

3. The Franchisor grants to the Franchisee the right to use its confidential know-how as set out more particularly in the Manuals and training courses. The Franchisee agrees, however, that any improvements and developments effected to such know-how by the Franchisee shall belong to the Franchisor to the benefit of the Franchisor and other Franchisees.

4. The Franchisor grants to the Franchisee the right to use the reputation and goodwill in the Wimpy name. The parties agree that any goodwill arising as a result of the carrying on by the Franchisee of the business of operating a Wimpy is the property of the Franchisor and the Franchisee shall execute and deliver to the Franchisor any documents considered necessary or desirable by the latter in connection with such goodwill.

B. Similar Business

1. The Franchisee agrees that during the term of this Agreement he shall not, either directly of indirectly, engage (as a franchisee or as a licensee) in any hamburger business in any form which is the same or similar to hamburger businesses as carried on pursuant to a license from the Franchisor.

2. The Franchisee further agrees that during the term of this Agreement he shall not, either directly or indirectly, engage or have an interest in any hamburger business which is the same or similar to the Franchisor's hamburger business without obtaining the prior written consent of the Franchisor.

C. Term

The Agreement shall commence on the date hereof and unless terminated in accordance with the terms and conditions hereof, shall remain in force for a period of ten (10) years.

3. Premises

The premises at which the Franchisee shall operate a Wimpy are described in the Schedule attached hereto. The Franchisee shall conduct business from the said Premises only if and when the Premises have been fitted out, decorated, furnished and equipped with restaurant equipment, furnishings and supplies which in the opinion of the Franchisor meet the Franchisor's specifications as described in the Manuals, and only for so long as the Premises continue to meet these specifications. All necessary consents under the Town and Country Planning Acts (or, where the Premises are situate in Scotland, the Town and Country Planning (Scotland) Acts) and local Authority Bye-Laws and Regulations and from any landlord, head landlord, owner or other person and all fire certificates and other necessary certificates and consents whatsoever shall have been obtained for the occupation and use by the Franchisee of the Premises for the purpose of operating the Wimpy. During the term of this Agreement, the Premises shall be used only by the Franchisee as solely for the purpose of operating a Wimpy according to the terms of this Agreement.

4. Training

The Franchisee himself or other person(s) designated by the Franchisee and agreed with the Franchisor involved in managing the Wimpy will attend the Franchisor's training school and Wimpy(s) designated by the Franchisor for training which Wimpy(s) shall be within a reasonable distance from the Premises for a period specified by the Franchisor which will normally be of 12 weeks duration and shall not operate a Wimpy until such time as he has completed such training to the satisfaction of the Franchisor. All expenses of travel, room, board and wages of the trainee shall be paid by the Franchisee. A significant part of the training will take place at a Wimpy approved by the Franchisor. If at any time any trainee shall voluntarily withdraw from training, or shall be unable to complete the training, or shall fail to demonstrate to the satisfaction of the Franchisor an aptitude, spirit or ability to comprehend and carry out the training as provided, then in such event the Franchisor shall have the right to require the Franchisee to appoint another trainee to undertake and successfully complete the training course.

5. Contribution: Sales: Accounting Procedures

A. Contribution

The Franchisee agrees in consideration of the Franchisor's licensing its use of the Trade Marks together with such other trade marks as may be authorised for use by the Franchisor, to pay a four-weekly contribution in the amount of $8\frac{1}{2}\%$ of Franchisee's Sales. The contributions shall be paid on or before the 10th day of each four-weekly period as defined by the Franchisor and shall be based upon Sales of the preceding four-weekly period, which Sales shall be evidenced by the appropriate cash register documentation. As a matter of internal accounting of the Franchisor these payments are divided into (i) a contribution to a National Advertising Fund which recognises the vital importance of advertising to the success of the Franchise, and which represents a significant proportion of such payments and (ii) a contribution to the costs incurred by the Franchisor in providing the services set out herein, and (iii) a contribution to the Franchisor's profit.

B. Sales

The term 'Sales' shall include the sale at or from the Premises of all goods, wares, merchandise or services of every kind, but shall exclude the amount of Sales from coin or token operated machines authorised by the Franchisor and any Value Added Tax or other similar tax which may now or hereafter be required to be paid by the Franchisee as against his Sales on the Premises. The Franchisee shall pay to the Franchisor any Value Added Tax chargeable upon the said payments of Contribution.

C. Accounting Procedures: Right of Audit

1. **Accounting Procedures** The Franchisee agrees to keep complete records of his business, and to prepare profit and loss statements for the Wimpy in accordance with the system of accounting described in the Manuals. The Franchisee shall provide to the Franchisor records of the Sales

and sales mixes of the Wimpy as may be requested from time to time by the Franchisor.

The Franchisee shall submit to the Franchisor a statement of Trading Profit of the Wimpy for each financial year of the Franchisee which shall be received by the Franchisor no later than twelve (12) weeks following the end of such year.

2. **Right of Audit** The Franchisee agrees that the Franchisor or its agents shall, at all reasonable times, have the right to examine or audit the books and accounts of the Franchisee to verify all figures as reported by the Franchisee.

6. Standards and Uniformity of Operation

The Franchisee agrees that the Franchisor's special standardised design and decor of buildings, uniformity of menu, equipment and layout, and adherence to the Manuals are essential to the image of a Wimpy. In recognition of the mutual benefits accruing from maintaining uniformity of appearance, service, products and marketing procedures, it is mutually covenanted and agreed:

A. Buildings and Premises

Except as specifically authorised by the Franchisor, the Franchisee shall not alter the appearance of the exterior or interior of the Premises. The Franchisee will maintain the Premises and will promptly make all repairs and alterations to the Wimpy and to the Premises as may reasonably be determined by the Franchisor to be necessary. Provided that if the Franchisor does not require any repairs or alterations as aforesaid it shall not be implied that the Premises are necessarily in a proper state of repair or construction.

B. Signs

The Franchisee agrees to display and maintain the Franchisor's Names, Trade Marks, and advertising and promotional material including posters, at the Premises, in the manner authorised by the Franchisor. The Franchisee agrees to maintain and display signs reflecting the then current image of the Franchisor. The colour, size, design and location of the said signs shall be as specified by the Franchisor. The Franchisee shall not place additional signs, posters or trade marks on the Premises other than those authorised by the Franchisor.

C. Equipment

The Franchisee agrees to obtain through the Franchisor and other approved sources by purchase or lease, machinery, equipment, furnishings and signs (hereinafter collectively called 'Equipment'). The list of Equipment which must be used by the Franchisee in the operation of his business is set out in the Manuals. The Franchisee agrees to maintain such Equipment in excellent working condition. As items of Equipment become obsolete or require to be replaced, the Franchisee will replace such items with either the same or substantially the same Equipment as is being installed in Wimpy at the time replacement becomes necessary. All Equipment used in the Franchisee's Wimpy shall meet the Franchisor's specifications.

D. Machines

No coin or token operated machines are to be installed in Wimpy unless authorised by the Franchisor.

E. Menu and Service

The Franchisee agrees to serve the Menu items specified in the Manuals to follow all specifications and formulae of the Franchisor, to sell no other food or drink item or any other merchandise of any kind without the prior written approval of the Franchisor. The Franchisee agrees that all food and drink items will be served in containers approved by the Franchisor bearing accurate reproductions of the Franchisor's Trade Marks. The Franchisor will establish approved sources of supply of Menu Items and other food and drink items and properly imprinted containers, and such items shall be purchased by the Franchisee through the Franchisor or such approved sources of supply.

The Franchisee agrees that it will operate its Wimpy in accordance with the standards, specifications and procedures set out in the Manuals. The Franchisee agrees further that changes in such standards, specifications and procedures may become necessary from time to time and agrees to accept such modifications, revisions and additions to the Manuals which the Franchisor in good faith and the exercise of its commercial judgement believes to be necessary. The Franchisee agrees not to deviate from the standards of cleanliness and sanitation as set by the Franchisor.

The Franchisee shall remain open for business daily between the hours of 10.00am and 11.00pm and any other hours as are agreed between the Franchisor and the Franchisee.

F. Alternative Suppliers

Where the Franchisee identifies a supplier of any items as an alternative to the Franchisor or its nominated supplier, the Franchisee agrees to obtain the written consent of the Franchisor before the use of such an alternative supplier in order to preserve the standards of quality, appearance, size, portion and taste as set out in the Manuals. The Franchisor shall require that samples from such an alternative supplier be delivered to the Franchisor and/or a designated independent testing laboratory for testing prior to approval and use, the costs of such testing to be shared equally between the Franchisor and Franchisee.

In the event that the Franchisor and/or its nominated supplier for any item(s), are unable or unwilling to supply such item(s), the Franchisee may obtain those item(s), but no others, from alternative suppliers for as long as the Franchisor and/or its nominated supplier shall be unable or unwilling so to supply.

G. Right of Entry and Inspection

The Franchisor or its authorised agent and representative shall have the right to enter and inspect the premises and examine and test and remove food products, supplies and equipment for the purpose of ascertaining that the Franchisee is operating the Wimpy in accordance with the terms of this Agreement and the Manuals. Inspection shall be conducted during normal business hours. The Franchisor shall notify the Franchisee of any deficiencies detected during inspection and the Franchisee shall forthwith correct any such deficiencies. Upon notification by the Franchisor that any equipment, food, supplies or imprinted containers do not meet the specifications, standards and requirements of the Franchisor, the Franchisee shall desist and refrain from the further use thereof.

7. Insurance Indemnification

A. The Franchisee agrees to obtain and pay premiums thereon for the term of this Franchise Agreement, a Public and Products Liability Policy, an Employers Liability Policy, and such other Policy as the Franchisor may stipulate, such policies to cover such amounts as are prudent for the operation at the Wimpy. The Franchisee agrees to name the Franchisor as an additional named insured (in the said policies) where appropriate and such policies shall stipulate that the Franchisor shall receive thirty (30) days written notice of cancellation or lapse. Original or duplicate copies of all insurance policies shall be furnished promptly to the Franchisor, together with proof of payment of the premiums thereof. All policies shall be renewed and evidence of renewal made available to the Franchisor.

B. The Franchisee is responsible for all loss or damage to third persons originating in or in connection with the operation of the Wimpy and for all claims or demands for damages to property or for injury, illness or death of persons directly or indirectly resulting therefrom, and the Franchisee agrees to defend, indemnify and save the Franchisor harmless of, from and with respect to any such claims, loss or damage, unless such claims, loss or damage result from the negligence of the Franchisor, its servants or agents.

8. Option at End of Term

Provided that the Franchisee shall have complied with all of the terms and conditions of this Agreement and shall have complied with the operating standards and criteria established for Wimpy, then at the expiration of the term hereof, the Franchisor will offer the Franchisee the opportunity to remain a Wimpy Franchisee for one additional period of   years, provided that:

A. The Franchisee shall agree to make such reasonable capital expenditure as may be required to renovate and modernise the Premises, signs and equipment so as to reflect the then current image of Wimpy.

B. The Franchisee has the right to remain in possession of the Premises, or in the event that the Franchisee elects (or is required) to relocate, other premises acceptable to the Franchisor for the new term.

C. The Franchisee shall execute a new Franchise Agreement in the form then being generally used by the Franchisor, except that no Franchise Payment payable under clause 1.A. hereof or its equivalent will be required.

D. The Franchisee shall give the Franchisor written notice of his desire to exercise his option to continue as a Franchisee not less than twelve (12) months prior to the expiration of the term of this Agreement.

9. Assignment: Conditions and Limitations

A. Subject to the provisions of paragraph B set out below the Franchisee shall not assign or grant any security over the benefits or obligations of this

Agreement nor purport so to do without the prior written consent of the Franchisor.

B. The Franchisee, his heirs or personal representatives, may sell and assign his rights under this Agreement to a bona fide purchaser. However before any such sale or assignment the Franchisee shall first offer to sell to the Franchisor on the same terms and conditions as offered to other prospective purchasers the business which is the subject of this Agreement. All offers shall be fully set forth in writing and the Franchisor shall have thirty (30) days within which to accept any such offer. If the Franchisor has not accepted such offer within thirty (30) days, the Franchisee may conclude the sale to the prospective purchaser upon such terms and conditions as aforesaid provided that the Franchisee is not in default hereunder and further provided that the Franchisor may impose reasonable conditions on any assignment permitted hereunder including but not limited to the following:

1. The Assignor must satisfy fully all obligations to the Franchisor or others arising out of the operation of the Wimpy or the Assignee must agree to assume and discharge all obligations to the Franchisor or others arising out of the operation of the Wimpy.

2. The Assignee must demonstrate to the satisfaction of the Franchisor that he meets at least the same financial and managerial criteria required of the Franchisee in qualifying for this Agreement.

3. The Assignee must agree to avail himself of the training required of new franchisees as hereinbefore set out in Clause 4.

4. The Assignee, prior to completion of the assignment, shall pay to the Franchisor the sum of one thousand pounds (£1,000) plus VAT as a contribution towards the cost of the assignment or the sum plus VAT representing the Franchisor's assignment fee current at the date of the assignment whichever is the higher.

5. The Assignor obtains a covenant on the part of the Assignee with the Franchisor to observe and perform all the terms and conditions of the Franchise Agreement.

10. Limitations of Franchise

A. Trade Marks, Trade Names and Trade Secrets

1. The Franchisee disclaims any right or interest in the Franchisor's Trade Marks and Trade Names or to the goodwill arrived therefrom subject to the provisions of Clause 2A herein. The Franchisee agrees that certain trade secrets, formulae, recipes and procedures may be made available to him in confidence and agrees not to divulge any such trade secrets, formulae, recipes and procedures or reproduce or exhibit any portion of the Manuals to any person other than his employees and further the Franchisee agrees to include a secrecy obligation relating to the above matters in any contract of employment with his employees.

2. The Franchisor shall have the right to terminate this Agreement forthwith in the event that the Franchisee questions, disputes, or attacks the validity, right, title or interest of the Franchisor as to the Franchisor's Trade Marks, Trade Names, patents, copyrights or other intellectual property rights.

The Franchisee shall immediately refer to the Franchisor (which shall have the sole right to defend the same) any threat or challenge to the Franchisor's Trade Marks, Trade Names, patents, copyrights or other intellectual property rights.

3. The Franchisee shall not incorporate in his trade name or trade style any trade mark of the Franchisor or any words confusingly similar thereto. Any display or use by the Franchisee of the Franchisor's Trade Marks and Trade Names shall be pursuant to the Franchisor's direction.

4. The Franchisee shall co-operate with the Franchisor to do all things that may be required to secure the registration of the Franchisee as a registered user of the Trade Marks in accordance with the provisions of the Trade Marks Act 1938.

5. The Franchisee shall not be entitled to exercise any of the rights relating to infringement conferred upon a registered user by Section 28(3) of the Trade Marks Act 1938.

B. No Agency

1. The parties hereto agree that the Franchisee is an independent contractor. Nothing herein contained shall constitute the Franchisee an agent, legal representative, partner, subsidiary, joint venturer or employee of the Franchisor. The Franchisee shall have no right or power to, and shall not bind or obligate the Franchisor in any way, manner or thing whatsoever, nor represent that he has any right to do so.

2. In all public records and in its relationship with other persons, on letterheads and business forms, the Franchisee shall indicate his independent ownership of the said business, and that he is a franchisee. The Franchisee agrees to exhibit on the Premises in a place and in a manner designated by the Franchisor, a notification that he is a franchisee of the Franchisor.

11. Default: Termination

A. Default

The occurrence of any of the following events shall constitute good cause for the Franchisor, at its option and without prejudice to any other rights or remedies provided for hereunder or by law or equity and without compensation, to terminate this Agreement by notice in writing to the Franchisee, such notice to expire at such date as the Franchisor in its absolute discretion determines:–

1. If the Franchisee is adjudicated bankrupt, has a receiving order made against him, calls a meeting of or makes any arrangement or composition with his creditors or has an attachment execution or distraint issued against or levied upon him or his effects, or (where the Franchisee is a partnership) any of the foregoing being done by or to the property of any of the partners of the Franchisee or the partnership being dissolved or (where the Franchisee is a body corporate) being unable to pay its debts within the meaning of Section 223 of the Companies Act 1948 as amended or having a Receiver or Manager appointed of any part of its undertaking or assets or uncalled capital, or an

order being made or a resolution being passed for winding up or liquidation of the Franchisee except where any such event is only for the purpose of amalgamation or reconstruction.

2. If the Franchisee defaults in the payment of contributions hereunder or in the payment of any other monies due to the Franchisor as a result of the operation of this Agreement or fails to submit profit and loss statements or other financial statements or data or reports on sales as provided herein or if the Franchisee makes any false statement in connection therewith.

3. If the Franchisee fails to maintain the standards as set forth in this Agreement, as may be supplemented by the Manuals.

4. If the Franchisee ceases to do business at the Premises or is in breach of any obligations under any lease or sublease or loses his right to the possession of the Premises.

5. If the Franchisee for any reason ceases to be entitled to remain registered as a registered user of any of the Trade Marks.

6. The Franchisee or any Manager being convicted during the term of this Agreement of any offence relating to the sale of alcoholic liquor or the use, abuse, sale, purchase or possession of drugs or narcotics, or theft, or fraud, or where the Franchisee is a partner in a firm, or a body corporate any person being so convicted who was, at the time of such conviction a partner in such firm or a director of such body corporate, or where the Franchisee carries out or knowingly permits to be carried out any activity on the Premises which in the unfettered opinion of the Franchisor would bring the Wimpy into bad repute.

7. If the Franchisee prepares, stores, advertises, or sells products other than Menu Items or ceases to carry out the preparation, storing, advertising and selling of Menu Items and any other products supplied by or with the authority of the Franchisor.

8. If the Franchisee fails to permit entry, inspection testing, examination or removal pursuant to Clause 6 G hereof.

B. Where the Franchisee is a body corporate the Franchisor shall also be entitled to terminate this Agreement, without compensation by giving written notice to the Franchisee in the event of:

(i) ceasing to be a Director of the body corporate

or (ii) a change of beneficial ownership of 50% or more of the shares

or (iii) a change in the voting control of the shares of the Franchisee

or (iv) a change in the composition of the Board of Directors of the Franchisee

or (v) the business of the Franchisee being merged with that of a third party

such notice shall be given to expire at any time up to three (3) months after the date that the Franchisor shall have knowledge of such an event.

C. Where the Franchisee commits any other breach of any of his obligations hereunder the Franchisor shall be entitled to terminate this Agreement at any time thereafter without compensation by giving thirty (30) days written notice to the Franchisee.

D. Effect of Termination

1. The Franchisee shall not after termination of this Agreement by lapse of time or upon default or for any other reason directly or indirectly identify himself in any manner as a former Wimpy franchisee. In particular, but without prejudice to the foregoing generality, the Franchisee shall not use any of the Franchisor's Trade Marks, Trade Names, signs, symbols, devices, insignia, or other distinctive materials, or any confusingly similar trade marks, trade names, signs, symbols, devices, insignia or other distinctive materials.

The Franchisee shall not, after termination of this Agreement, use any trade secrets, recipes, formulae or other materials of the Franchisor. Such prohibition is, however, without prejudice to the right of the Franchisor to make such lump sum or royalty charge as it considers reasonable in the circumstances for the use of such trade secrets, recipes, formulae or other materials in respect of a period not exceeding three (3) years from the date of termination.

The Franchisee grants to the Franchisor the option to purchase all paper goods, containers, signs, menus and any and all insignia bearing the Franchisor's Trade Name or Marks thereon at the higher of cost or fair market value at the time of termination and the same shall be delivered to the Franchisor at the expense of the Franchisee.

2. The Franchisee agrees that, upon termination of this Agreement by lapse of time or upon default, he will immediately remove all references to the Franchisor's Trade Marks, Trade Names and insignia as the Franchisor shall request in order to distinguish effectively the Premises from their former appearance and from any other Wimpy. If the Franchisee shall fail to make such changes forthwith, then the Franchisor may enter upon the Franchisee's Premises and make such changes at the Franchisee's expense.

3. In the event of termination by reason of default of the Franchisee, the extent of all damage which the Franchisor has suffered by virtue of such default shall be and remain a lien in favour of the Franchisor against any and all of the personal property, machinery, fixtures and equipment owned by the Franchisee on the premises at the time of such default.

4. Termination of the Agreement for any reason shall not release either party hereto from any obligation which at the date of termination has already accrued to the other party (whether or not the amount of such liability has been computed) or which under the terms hereof or by its nature is a continuing obligation.

12. Miscellaneous: General Conditions

A. Interpretation

The Recitals and the Schedules are incorporated in and made a part of this Agreement. Titles of clauses and paragraphs are used for convenience only and are not a part of the text. All terms used in any one gender shall be construed to include any other gender as the context may require. The singular shall be deemed to include the plural and the plural shall be deemed to refer to the singular as the context may require. If the Franchisee is more than one (1) in number all rights and obligations of the Franchisee shall be joint and several.

B. Entire Agreement

This Agreement constitutes the entire Agreement between the parties and shall prevail over any other agreement relating to the subject matter hereof except where the Franchisor is the Franchisee's landlord of the Premises, in which event the lease of the Premises shall be construed independently of the Agreement and vice versa. The Franchisee declares that he relies upon no representations, conditions or warranties on the part of the Franchisor except as herein contained.

C. Non-Waiver

The failure of the Franchisor to exercise any right, power or option given to it hereunder, or to insist upon strict compliance with the terms hereof by the Franchisee shall not constitute a waiver of the terms and conditions of this Agreement with respect to that or any other or subsequent breach thereof, nor a waiver by the Franchisor of its rights at any time thereafter to require exact strict compliance with all the terms hereof. The rights or remedies hereunder are cumulative to any other rights or remedies which may be granted by law.

D. Governing Law

This Agreement shall be governed and construed in accordance with the laws of England.

E. Severability

If any provision of this Agreement is held invalid by court decree, such a finding shall not invalidate the remainder of this Agreement.

F. Notices

Any notice to be given hereunder shall be in writing and shall be deemed to have been duly served if sent by first class pre-paid post addressed to the party to be served at its above written address or its last known place of business.

G. Employees

The staff employed at the Premises shall remain at all times the employees of the Franchisee. However, the Franchisee will be expected to conform with the code of conduct and standards set out in the Manuals.

IN WITNESS WHEREOF:
THE COMMON SEAL OF WIMPY INTERNATIONAL LIMITED was hereunto affixed in the presence of

Director

Director

The Schedule

The Premises

8
Methods of trading

The franchisor is practically always a limited company. Your research will show you whether the company is sound and whether the franchisor has the resources to carry out the services promised.

You will have to decide in what capacity to sign the agreement and trade; you could sign the agreement personally as a sole trader or as a partnership or as a limited liability company. If you sign as a limited liability company the franchisor will almost definitely require you (and your partners, if any) to sign the agreement personally to guarantee the performance of the company. This chapter deals with the following methods of trading and the tax implications:
* Sole trader.
* Setting up a partnership – advantages and disadvantages.
* Setting up a company – advantages and disadvantages.

Sole trader

As a sole trader you alone will be responsible for the business. You will be able to employ other people under the PAYE system. Most small businesses start trading as a sole trader and later become a limited company.

Caution: You will be entitled to all the profits, but should the business fail you alone will be responsible personally for all the debts and may well risk losing all your personal possessions including your house. As a sole trader you will need to do the following:

Keep proper records
Your franchisor will usually have a rigid system of monitoring your sales and will oblige you to use a particular system of accounting. Good housekeeping is essential to the success of any business. In addition it will be very important for VAT and tax reasons; the Customs and Excise and the Inland Revenue may wish to inspect your records at any time. A tax inspector will have a field day if your records are bad.

VAT
Initially you should contact your local VAT office and arrange an appointment with the VAT officer who will be able to advise you fully as to which rules apply to your business. Depending on your projected turnover figures you may have to register for VAT. It is very important that you consider the VAT implications on your cash flow and profit figures – they make a significant difference but most franchisors do not take them into account.

Employees
If you are going to employ staff, whether full-time or part-time, you will need to acquaint yourself with the PAYE returns and various forms of legislations, e.g. sick pay, maternity leave, sex discrimination. Don't panic. Everyone is extremely helpful. The PAYE returns office will assist you in how to calculate wages and National Insurance contributions and tax for your employees. Once you have got the hang of using the tables and filling in the forms you will realize how easy it is, providing you keep up-to-date. The DHSS is very helpful in advising about legislation and various leaflets on the subject are also available.

Setting up a partnership

You may want to set up a partnership for a number of reasons, e.g. division of labour or injection of money. The most successful partnerships tend to be between husband and wife or family members. It is normally said that the best way to lose a good friend is to go into partnership with them. There is a lot of truth in this but if that is what you want to do for whatever reason then you should carefully consider the implications of a partnership.

A business partnership is an association of two or more people (up to twenty) trading together as one firm and sharing the profits. A tax assessment is made on the profits of the partnership. The partners are responsible for the obligations of each other, so if one partner fails to pay tax the others will have to pay it. It is very important that you have a partnership agreement drawn up by a solicitor stating exactly what you and your partner have agreed, e.g. the share of profits, what happens if a partner wishes to leave or dies or a new partner comes in, conditions of termination, voting rights, holiday leave and who are signatories on cheques. Partnerships that go wrong are a nightmare and every situation should be covered by the agreement.

Sleeping partner
This is a partner who just puts in money, but takes no part in the day to day running of the business.

Ordinary partnership and the limited partnership
Two types of partnership exist. The ordinary partnership and the rare limited partnership. A limited partner cannot participate in the day to day running of the business and is only liable up to the amount of capital he contributes. A limited partnership must have at least one unlimited or general partner who has unlimited joint and several liability. He may be held responsible for all the firm's debts.

Trading name
Sole traders and partnerships can trade under their own name or names or under another name or title. If the trading name is not their own surname(s) then the name(s) of the owners must be stated on stationery and displayed at the office, shop or place of work.

Public inspection
A partnership's financial affairs are not available for public inspection.

Income tax: Sole Traders and Partnerships
All the business profits are treated as sole trader's or partner's income and taxed accordingly under Schedule D.
   REMEMBER, THE MAJOR DISADVANTAGE OF TRADING AS A SOLE TRADER OR AS A PARTNERSHIP IS THAT YOUR LIABILITY IS UNLIMITED. YOU WILL BE PERSONALLY LIABLE FOR ALL THE DEBTS OF THE BUSINESS.

Your accounting year
Accounts are made up annually. However, the first trading period may be longer for a sole trader or partnership. It is up to you to decide which day is to be your year's end. Some people use the end of the Tax Year, i.e. April 5th. Discuss the matter with your accountant. He will suggest a date which will give you the longer period for paying your taxes which will normally mean a year from 30th April.

Claiming allowances
It is in your interests that these are quickly and correctly claimed. The inspector of taxes will want to see the firm's trading account, profit and loss account and perhaps the balance sheet. He may also ask for invoices, receipts, bank records etc., and it is strongly advised that you have an accountant to deal with the matter. He is an expert and will know exactly what the inspector wants.

Allowances on capital expenditure
Money spent on plant, buildings, machinery, vehicles and other things that benefit the business and do not have to be renewed every year are called capital expenditure. Allowances are given for this type of expenditure. For a sole trader these allowances are set off against

income for tax purposes. Before making any expenditure it is wise to check with your accountant to find out whether it will qualify for the annual writing down allowance.

Deductible expenses

Those expenses which are incurred wholly and exclusively in the performance of the duties of your business can be set off against tax. Some of these are:
– expenses of business travel, but not travelling expenses from home to work. Travelling expenses on business journeys are allowed together with the cost of subsistence when away from home.
– an allowance for the upkeep of tools and special clothing is allowed, but not normal clothing even if you would not wear it outside work.
– if you have to work from home then you will be able to claim a proportion of the cost of lighting, heating, telephone etc.
– wages of wife employed in the business; however she will have to be included in the husband's tax return.
– interest on business loans.
– interest charges on hire-purchase of capital equipment.
– hire or leasing of equipment.
– insurance premiums.
– bad debts.
– entertainment for *overseas* customers.
– subscriptions to trade and professional associations.
– cost of self-employed retirement annuity.

If you have a business car you will be able to claim the running costs as a deductible expense so make sure you keep a record of the business mileage as well as the total mileage.

Tax deductible losses

A sole trader's or partnership's losses may be offset against any income that the trader or his wife may receive from other sources in that year or the next. In addition one of the biggest benefits of trading as a sole trader or partnership is that any losses in the first four years can be offset against wages or other income received in the three years *before* the trading started. So in effect you will be getting back a part of the tax you had previously paid.

If you were in the position where you hadn't previously paid much tax then you could carry the losses forward to future business years and offset against future profits.

Assessment of income tax

Special rules are applied to the first three years.

First tax year   – Tax is assessed on profits from the first day of trading up to 5th April. Where the accounting year ends at a later date a proportion is calculated on a time basis.

Second tax year – Income Tax is assessed on the profits of the first twelve months of trading. Again, apportionment may be necessary.

Third tax year – Income Tax is assessed on the accounting year ending in the previous tax year.

Optional assessment

In the second and third year of trading you could elect to be assessed on the *actual* profits made in those years. Obviously only do that if the profits for whatever reason are lower in these years than in your first trading period.

The tax assessment situation in a sole trader or partnership is extremely beneficial to you because you can end up paying little or no tax – simply because the first twelve months profits which you should keep low are the basis for two or even three years' tax bills.

When is the tax payable?

Income tax is payable in two instalments – due on 1st January and 1st July. This is why it is extremely important that you choose a good accounting date, e.g. if you choose a day in May as the end of your trading period then that is one month after the end of the tax year, so you won't be assessed for tax for about a year after your annual accounts are made up and you won't actually have to pay tax until the following January and July. This is great because you will not be paying anything to the Inland Revenue for about two years!

Setting up a limited company

A limited company is treated like an individual person – a legal entity in its own right. Therefore you and the company are totally separate. Rules of company law apply and these are contained in the Companies Acts.

Shareholders

There have to be at least two shareholders and they will be responsible for the company's debts to the value of the shares they hold. Thus, their liability is said to be limited. This is the protection that a limited company gives you but you must be careful when signing the franchise contract or any agreement because you will only have limited liability if you sign in the name of the company. If you sign in your own capacity or give an additional personal guarantee then you will be held responsible for all the debts.

Public or private
A limited company can be public (plc) or private. When a company is public, shares can be brought by members of the public and the company may be quoted on the Stock Exchange. Private companies, on the other hand, do not offer shares to the public and they state limited after their name.

Registering a company
In England and Wales you will have to register a limited company with the Registrar of Companies. A number of formalities must be complied with and the following submitted:

Memorandum of association
This details the name of the company, the country in which it is registered, the company's objects, statement of the limited liability of its members, the amount of share capital and the way in which it is divided into shares. It must be signed and witnessed.

Articles of association
These cover the internal matters of the company. For example, the powers of the directors. There are other forms that will have to be filled in on registration and a fee will be payable.

Off the shelf company
You can buy a company 'off the shelf' through a company registration agent. Basically, this is a non-operating company which has been registered by the agent. After you have bought it your names will be substituted for the original names. The name of the company can be kept or changed depending on you. The cost of buying an off the shelf company is around £125.

Accounting records
Minimum accounting requirements for limited companies are laid down by the Companies Act 1976. The accounting records must:
* Disclose with reasonable accuracy the financial position of the company.
* Enable the directors to ensure that the balance sheet and profit and loss account they have prepared give a true and fair view of the company's state of affairs.

Limited companies must prepare audited annual accounts. Therefore you will have to employ the services of an accountancy firm. You will note that the accounts of sole traders or partnerships do not have to be audited.

Tax considerations
Companies pay corporation tax and usually make up accounts for a

twelve month period to an accounting reference date which you can select. If you do not select a date then you are assigned the standard accounting reference date of 31st March. The twelve month period is called the corporation tax accounting period and the tax due on taxable trading income of this period is due about nine months after the end of the corporation tax accounting period.

Directors

As a director of a limited company you are treated as an employee and therefore you will pay income tax on your salary under the PAYE system. Under the PAYE system you will pay the salary to yourself having deducted national insurance and tax which you send to the Inland Revenue. You can choose to do this weekly, monthly or once a year if the Inland Revenue agree. If at the end of the year there is a profit this can be divided between the directors as additional salary and tax will be deducted. If the profit is not taken out as salary it will be liable for corporation tax.

Professional advice

It is very important that you consult an accountant for advice on whether to take out profits as salary or to leave them in the company and pay corporation tax.

Corporation tax – Limited companies

As explained previously this is the tax that companies pay on their profits. There are two rates which the following table will clarify:-

	1986–1987
Full rate 35%	Reduced small company rate 29%
Annual profit – £500,000 35% is applied on *all* profits (i.e. the full rate is applied even to the profits below £100,000)	Annual profits £100,000 Up to £100,000 29% is applied and above this it gradually increases according to a formula

Capital allowances and losses of a limited company

These are the same in the case of sole traders, partnerships and limited companies but they can only be offset against the company's income.

Trading loss

Trading losses can be set off against the previous years' profits but must be claimed within two years. They can also be carried forward and offset against future profits but these claims must be made within six years.

Sole Trader/Partnership or Company

Having carefully digested this chapter you may still be unsure as to how to trade. To help you further here is a summary of the important considerations.

Sole trader/ *Partnership*	*Company*
1) May not have to pay tax for up to two years.	Tax payable – 9 months after the profits.
2) Money may be drawn from the business without a tax cost.	income tax is payable on any money drawn out.
3) Tax losses can be offset against the proprietor's other income.	A company tax loss *cannot* be offset against the proprietor's other income.
4) Assessment rules are very beneficial and the commencement and cessation provisions can result in certain income escaping tax.	There are no special assessment provisions.
5) Profits can be attributed to a partner's spouse if that spouse is in the partnership, and this means their personal allowances can be used.	Usually a spouse of the director/shareholder has to work full-time in the business before a deduction can be secured.
6) Expenses incurred 'wholly and exclusively' are deductible.	Expenses incurred 'wholly and exclusively' for the company's trade are deductible but if they benefit the director a taxable benefit in kind arises and the director will have to pay income tax *unless* he can show that the expense was incurred 'wholly, exclusively and necessarily' for the purposes of his employment as director.
7) Losses in the first four years of trading can be carried back three years against other income.	A loss attributable to first year allowances can be carried back three years. Other losses can only be carried back one year against the company's income only.

8)	Capital Gains Tax is payable by the partners.	A double charge to CGT could arise – when an asset is sold by the company and when the shares are sold or the company is liquidated.
9)	Relief is available on the sale of the partnership business and assets including goodwill.	No relief is available on the sale of shares in a company.
10)	The partners are completely liable for the debts of the business.	Limited liability.
11)	A partner may bind all the other partners. A partnership is not a separate entity.	A company is a separate legal entity.
12)	Maximum of twenty partners except for solicitors, accountants and stockbrokers.	Minimum of two shareholders.
13)	Partners can withdraw capital as they have agreed.	Withdrawal of capital restricted by company law.
14)	Auditing of accounts not required by law.	Audited accounts required by law.
15)	Accounts do not have to be filed.	Accounts have to be filed with the Registrar of Companies.

9
Closing down

If you go into business and everything goes wrong, what can you expect to happen? Having devoted the previous chapter to 'setting up the business', it is essential that the reader should be aware of what happens if all does not go according to plan.

Everybody goes into business to succeed. But unfortunately no business is risk free. Every businessman/woman should know what to do if things start going wrong. Most people panic. This is one time when you must stay calm. It helps to know what is going on and to remember that there is no shame in 'failing'. Some of the most successful people are where they are because they learn from their experiences and persevere. Deal with the situation as efficiently as possible and then carry on with your life positively. Never regard the incident as a 'failure'. It is an experience, and you may rest assured that your solicitor and accountant will be able to deal with everything effectively.

An individual is usually referred to as having gone 'bankrupt' while a company goes into 'liquidation'. In reality the expression means the same thing. When a company goes into liquidation it will start selling all its assets in order to convert everything into cash and satisfy the outstanding debts to its creditors. If you are in the position where even if you sell all your assets you cannot cover your debts you have gone bankrupt. In effect you or your company have died a financial death.

You can make yourself or your company bankrupt or a creditor can put you into a state of bankruptcy. However most creditors will want you to continue trading because then they are more likely to recover their debts. Your debts and assets will be passed on to the official receiver and he will act as your 'executor' or will appoint a trustee to act for you. The official receiver sells everything and pays off all the creditors that he can.

Bankruptcy

Ordinary bankruptcy –   where you or your company get into debt as a result of genuine difficulties the official receiver will deal with everything quickly and quietly.

Criminal bankruptcy – if there has been any fraud or crime or you have deliberately gone out of your way to swindle your creditors you could be fined or imprisoned.

The county court order

A formal notice will be sent to you advising you of the claim against you. The form will give you three alternatives and fourteen days to act. If you don't answer the registrar will make an order in your absence.

The three alternatives

1) Acknowledge the debt – pay in full or offer to pay in fourteen days.
2) Acknowledge the debt and say on reverse of form that you can't pay but are prepared to pay monthly. The creditor can accept your terms and then you will be notified of when to start the instalments. If he doesn't accept your terms you will be notified of the date of the hearing.
3) Deny the whole or part of the debt.

The hearing is private and you may come to an agreement with the creditor before the actual hearing. If you haven't come to an agreement the registrar will make an order for instalments. If you can't meet the payments you will be able to apply for a reduction in the payments. This application could be granted or refused. You will be required to pay the instalments direct to the court unless you have a special arrangement allowing payment to the creditor. *If you don't pay* the court won't do anything until the creditor applies for a bailiff's warrant for non-payment.

The high court writ

A writ will be served on you. You or your solicitor will need to acknowledge it. Even if you agree that you will pay by instalments the creditor can at any time decide to have your goods seized by the bailiff.

The bailiff and the warrant

A court bailiff will deliver the warrant to you. The order will require you to pay the outstanding amount. He will tell you to contact your solicitor immediately and meet the debt or your goods will be seized. Remember the bailiff is only doing his job so don't get irate with him. They don't particularly want to take all your goods – they would rather you eventually paid and will usually be prepared to wait a few extra days for you to do just that.

The bailiff cannot take anything belonging to someone else, for instance, goods belonging to a supplier, but the owner has to sign a statement saying that the goods belong to him. If he isn't around to sign the goods will be taken and you will have to inform him that his goods have been taken by the bailiff and give him the bailiff's phone number and a reference number. He will be able to reclaim his goods before they are auctioned. A list of the goods taken will be made and you will be asked to sign a statement. Any goods that are not reclaimed by other people, e.g. suppliers – will be auctioned. The bailiff will take out costs of the warrant and collection of goods and the remainder will go towards paying your debt.

Time with the receiver

You will spend about a week with the receiver. You will be involved in listing debts and assets and compiling a short life story of your trading. An inspector (assistant to the receiver) will take all your books, statements, invoices, accounts etc. He will also fill in forms on your behalf. Cooperate with him as much as possible – he is trying to help you. Everything is being done so that the official receiver knows that you are not hiding anything. His job is to establish the cause of your bankruptcy and to prepare a statement. It's going to feel like forever. But don't despair. Get the formalities out of the way quickly.

The statement
You will sign the statement and the receiver's inspector will sign as your witness. A shortened version of the statement will be drafted by the inspector and sent to your creditors with a formal notice of your bankruptcy. They will be asked to inform the receiver of how much your debt to them is and they will be notified of the creditors meeting and the public hearing date and invited to attend.

Notices
One notice is put in the London Gazette and the other in a local paper.

The creditors' meeting

Every creditor is entitled to attend in person or send a representative or to appoint the official receiver as a proxy. The idea of doing this is to enable the creditors to get together and raise any questions. While the meeting is taking place you will have to be present in the building but you don't actually have to be at the meeting. Try to be at the meeting if you can because then you can answer questions that creditors may raise.

The vote
The creditors will be asked to vote as to whether one of their number should be appointed as a trustee in bankruptcy, i.e. someone responsible for overseeing the sale of your assets and distribution to creditors. Alternatively they may decide to appoint a solicitor or accountant. Whatever they decide the official receiver remains in charge.

Fees
Whoever is appointed becomes a preferential creditor and will be paid from your assets.

The trustee
If a trustee is appointed at the creditors' meeting he will be responsible for selling your assets. He is responsible for the creditors' interests.

The public hearing

You will have to attend this at the local County Court. It can be a harrowing experience but once this is over you can put it all behind you. The press, public and creditors are allowed in and they can ask you questions in open court.

Public hearing dispensation
Where you have been upfront and honest with the official receiver he can apply to have the public hearing dispensed with. The registrar makes his judgement and from this point you are adjudged bankrupt. The judgement could be:
* Adjudged bankrupt with an automatic discharge after five years.
* Adjudged bankrupt with a promise to call you back in five years when you will get a discharge if you can show that you have not got into further financial problems.
* Adjudged bankrupt forever.

Summary – timetable of events

Day 1	You go to official receiver or creditor goes to him and declares you bankrupt.
Day 2	Inspector and valuer visit you and value assets.
Weeks 1, 2	Spend about a week with the official receiver's inspector.
Weeks 3, 4	Official announcement to creditors in the press.
Week 6	Creditors meeting.
Week 10	Public hearing attended but postponed.
Week 13	Public hearing application.

The whole thing takes about thirteen weeks. Once it's all over, have a rest and try to forget about it. Above all be positive and don't blame yourself. The experience, although often traumatic, could prove to be invaluable to you in the future. Don't forget there is a risk factor in every business.

In franchising your business may have failed due to circumstances beyond your control and you may well need to seek advice from a solicitor in relation to legal claims against your franchisor and possibly other parties.

Creditors

Your creditors fall into one of four categories:

Fully secured creditors
This type of creditor is secured against a particular asset, e.g. the bank in relation to your house. The bank will be able to sell your house and obtain their monies. If they obtain more than is owed to them they have to hand it over to the official receiver. If they don't obtain enough to cover their debt they become an unsecured creditor. In most cases the bank will not want to turn you out of your home – especially when there are children involved. Usually they will come to an arrangement with you whereby you will have to undertake to obtain a full-time job and pay off the outstanding debt in instalments.

Partly secured creditors
Here the creditor is aware of what amount is fully secured and what amount is unsecured right from the start. Example:
    You borrow £5,000
    You sign over stocks and shares to the value of £4,600
    The creditor is fully secured for £4600
    The creditor is unsecured for £400
If he manages to sell the stocks and shares for *more* the rest goes to the official receiver. If he doesn't even manage to reclaim his own secured monies then he can increase the unsecured amount.

Preferential creditors
After all the secured loans are paid, if there is any remaining money it is paid to the preferential creditors. These are:
– The trustee in bankruptcy's fees, official receiver's fees, rates, Inland Revenue, VAT, National insurance and staff wages.
– If there is enough money they are *all paid*. However, if there isn't enough they all get a percentage of their own debt.

– Wages will be paid by the government who then becomes a creditor for the money.

Unsecured creditors
Everybody else to whom you owe money is an unsecured creditor. Whatever, if any, money is available at the end will be paid to the unsecured creditors again as a percentage of their debt.
   Note: It is **illegal** for you to pay a particular creditor in preference to another.

Receivership liquidations

When a company runs out of cash one talks of liquidation rather than bankruptcy. Often when a company is experiencing cash flow problems a receiver is appointed where the company has granted a debenture. If a receiver cannot be appointed the company will eventually go into liquidation.

Legislation
Most of the relevant legislation is contained in the Companies Act of 1984 and the Insolvency Act of 1986.

Receivership
When a receiver is appointed under a debenture he takes control of the company assets and the floating charge is turned into a fixed charge. The company still exists but directors, shareholders and creditors have not got any rights and cannot do a lot. A receiver does not have to have contact with shareholders or creditors but in most cases they do try to be very helpful and keep everybody informed of what is going on.

Who can put the company into receivership?
*   Either the company itself
*   or a secured bank or debenture holder or unsecured creditor.
Note: A floating charge must exist for a receiver to be appointed. If it doesn't exist then liquidation is the only alternative.

What is a floating charge?
This is a charge or security which allows the company to use its assets freely while it is trading normally *but* when the charge becomes enforceable the floating charge is said to have 'crystallized' and the company can no longer continue to deal freely with its assets.

Where does the receiver derive his authority from?
*   The receiver is usually appointed the agent of the company and his decisions are binding.
*   The receiver acts for the benefit of the debenture holder.

Receiver's powers
The extent of a receiver's powers are as follows:
 1) To collect in and sell the assets.
 2) Management of the business.
 3) Arrange insurances.
 4) Come to compromises.
 5) Sell assets to a subsidiary.
 6) Incorporate a subsidiary.
 7) Employ staff.
 8) To grant leases.
 9) To borrow money.
10) To exercise powers of attorney.
11) To bring and defend proceedings in the name of the company.
   The receiver has no duty to unsecured creditors. He acts for the benefit of the debenture holder but note when the assets are realized that the preferential creditors have priority over the debenture holder where the floating charge has crystallized.

Types of receiver
A receiver can be appointed by the Court or by the holder of a fixed or floating charge.

An official receiver
An official receiver is appointed by the Department of Trade and is an officer of the court to which he is attached. An official receiver doesn't usually act as receiver of a company (unless he is appointed by the court because he is already liquidator of that company). Normally the official receiver acts as liquidator and then he is called the Official Receiver and Liquidator.

Liquidations

There are two types of liquidation – voluntary and compulsory. When a company is insolvent it goes into liquidation, i.e. the company's existence is ended.

Voluntary liquidation

A liquidator is appointed by the shareholders of a company and its creditors.

Procedure
*   Company becomes insolvent.

* Extraordinary resolution is passed by the *shareholders* to appoint and nominate a liquidator.
* Creditors' meeting arranged almost immediately. The creditors can replace the liquidator chosen by the shareholder by obtaining the support of the majorities of creditors present in person or by proxy. This must be satisfied in value of the claim.

Format of meeting

The directors explain reasons for the company failing and then the creditors can ask questions. Votes will then be taken as to which liquidator is to be appointed. This can be a very noisy and frantic period as there may be serious arguments as to choice of liquidator. The liquidator will usually be more biased towards helping the party that appointed him and therefore each side wants their own liquidator.

Liquidator's powers

After the vote has taken place the liquidator is officially in office and his powers are as per section 245, Companies Act of 1948:

1) to bring and defend proceedings.
2) to carry on the business of the company as far as is necessary for winding it up.
3) to appoint a solicitor.
4) to pay dividends to creditors.
5) to compromise claims by creditors and against shareholders.
6) to sell assets.
7) to give receipts and use the company's seal.
8) to prove in other insolvencies.
9) to draw or endorse bills.
10) to borrow money on the security of assets.
11) to appoint agents.
12) to do everything necessary for winding up the company's affairs.

Compulsory liquidation

Here the company or a creditor presents a petition to the court to make a compulsory winding up order. The petition gives a description of the company and states the reasons why it should be wound up. Petitions can be presented in the High Court or County Court. In cases of public interest the Department of Trade can present a petition.

The petition is heard by a judge a few weeks later and he can make a compulsory winding up order. If such an order is made it is effective retrospectively from the date of presentation of the petition. When the order is made the Official Receiver becomes provisional liquidator. He arranges for a report on the company and a statement of its affairs and convenes a creditors' meeting.

The creditors' meeting
Votes are cast for a liquidator and committee of inspection. The Official Receiver reports on the results of the voting to the Companies Court and they then appoint a liquidator to replace the Official Receiver, and appoint a committee of inspection. Where no decision can be reached the Official Receiver continues as liquidator without a committee.

Comparison of receivership and liquidation

A receivership is not as traumatic as a liquidation. A receiver will not usually close down the business and indeed may be active in negotiating a sale. Once liquidation starts the company will cease to exist.

Powers of receivers and liquidators differ. A company can be in receivership and liquidation at the same time and if this is the case the receiver's powers are lessened but he can still realize assets falling with the floating charge and he can still account to the debenture holder.

Directors' responsibilities during insolvency
Once the directors realize that their company is insolvent they must consider receivership or liquidation. If they don't they might be subjecting themselves to civil and criminal penalties.

It is clear from company legislation that if you know your company is insolvent you *must* stop trading. The courts do, however, take a sympathetic view where you continue to trade genuinely thinking that you can improve the situation – but you need to be very careful.

What is manifestly wrong is if directors allow a company to incur credit at a time when the business is being carried on in such circumstances that it is clear that the company will never be able to satisfy its creditors. However, there is nothing to say that directors who genuinely believe that the clouds will roll away and the sunshine of prosperity will shine upon them again and disperse the fog of their depression are not entitled to incur credit to help them get over the bad time.

The above ruling is called the 'sunshine' test, but remember you must act with the greatest of caution when continuing to trade and you must obtain the independent advice of an accountant. Then you must ensure that you heed the accountant's advice, especially if he advises that you cease trading.

Fraudulent preferences
Finally, if your business is experiencing difficulties and you are being pressurized by some creditors to pay them – *don't*!! Where your unsecured creditors are concerned you must treat them all the same. Any payment to one creditor in preference to another (even if you

think that eventually they will all be paid) is a fraudulent preference and the liquidator may want to recover such sums in the liquidation.

What you need to do
Above all, stay cool. Do not fraudulently prefer any creditor. If your stock can be returned to suppliers then write to them explaining the situation and arrange for them to collect their stock; this will at least reduce your debt to them. Insist that *they* collect. You haven't the funds to arrange deliveries if you are going insolvent!

Some creditors may threaten to wind you up but if you are going into liquidation anyway – don't worry about it. There is nothing you can do. Put the entire matter into the hands of your solicitor. Above all, keep all your creditors, your bank and your solicitor informed of everything that is going on.

10

Problems of unfair and fraudulent trading

Franchising can be an extremely good way of doing business for everyone concerned. However, unfortunately it is very easy for unfair and fraudulent practices to develop within it. For example, fictitious data may be provided to induce potential franchisees to sign the contract. The reader should be aware that this can go on and should be on his guard. LOOK OUT for the following:
1) Fictitious data – e.g. market research.
2) Fictitious accounting information.
3) Non-existent pilot schemes.
It is not just the cowboys who have done this. Sometimes reputable international names have been involved.

In some cases royalty payments have been presented as low and the franchisor has made extortionate mark-ups on tied products. In other cases, franchisees have been told there would be no mark-ups when in fact there were.

Sales projections may be distorted and should be carefully analysed. Remember that projections comprise *estimated* figures for *illustrative* purposes only. They are not the same as forecasts.

A franchisor is supposed to provide the franchisee with expertise and training. In some cases the training is quite inadequate or even abysmal, and the operating manual worthless – yet another reason why the franchisor should be asked detailed questions as outlined previously, and the franchisee should ensure that he is indeed dealing with experienced experts.

You should also ensure that the franchisor spends advertising money correctly. In some cases the franchisor's only interest has been to raise more capital by advertising for more franchisees. Thus, they have been collecting 'franchise fees' rather than making money by trading. This is simply Pyramid Selling and is illegal. Be wary of the franchisor who glowingly tells you how many units they intend to have by the end of the year – maybe he is just more interested in opening other units than ensuring that each outlet is successful. Franchisors who pursue such a policy will then only wish to retain the profitable units and you will find that they then pursue a policy of getting rid of other franchisees. This can be quite easily achieved by making life very difficult for the franchisee. The franchisor can withhold sufficient services and support and supply the franchisee with inferior products or stock while supplying company-owned shops with good stock. This will inevitably affect the franchisee's sales and may lead to a situation whereby the franchisee wants to leave the franchise voluntarily.

If the franchisee does not leave voluntarily the franchisor may terminate the contract. This can be done quite easily as a termination clause will be present. Often they seize upon some trivial breach of the contract as an excuse to terminate.

Another ruse used is to withhold supplies. Obviously a franchisee cannot flourish without stock. If the franchisor is acting wrongly in doing this the franchisee will be able to bring an action.

At the present time there is no specific franchise legislation, although there is a growing body of people who feel that the time has come for such legislation in our system. Thus the usual principles of general law apply plus the regulations of the British Code of Advertising Practice established by the Advertising Standards Association (ASA). Where the franchisor is fraudulent our criminal system can deal with it adequately. The problems arise when the franchisor uses sharp and unfair practices.

British Code of Advertising Practice

This is a self-regulating system supervised by the ASA. The chairman is appointed from outside the advertising industry and about half its members have no connection with advertising. The committee concerned with the day to day running of the organization consists of representatives of advertising organizations, agencies and the media. Pre-publication guidance can be obtained.

Object of the Code
To ensure that all advertisements are legal, decent, honest and truthful and show responsibility to the consumer and conform to the principles of fair competition as generally accepted in business. Advertisements should not abuse the trust of consumers or exploit their lack of expertise. Descriptions and claims in advertisements should be genuine and capable of being substantiated.

Consumer complaints
These are investigated by the Code of Advertising Practice Committee (CAP) and the Advertising Standards Association Secretariat which reports to the ASA. The ASA publishes details of the complaints, whether they have been upheld and the names of advertisers involved. Any advertisement found to be a breach of the code is not published by

the media adherents and neither will they accept advertisements from agencies which defy the ASA's authority. In franchising you should be aware that it is arguable that statements such as: 'Be your own boss' or a 'business of your own' are misleading and do infringe the code. Misleading statements about the true rate of royalty payments would also be a breach of the code.

Television and radio advertising
This is monitored by the Independent Broadcasting Authority (IBA) constituted under the Independent Broadcasting Authority Act 1973. Standards and practice are set out in the IBA Code and are similar to those contained in the Code of Advertising Practice. If the reader feels that any advertisement is genuinely misleading he should not hesitate to lodge a complaint.

Misrepresentation and remedies

Where misrepresentations of fact are made by the franchisor, his servants or agents – and these can relate to anything, whether written or oral representations – the Misrepresentation Act 1967 applies. Damages would probably be awarded in cases of fraudulence. Where however, the misrepresentation is merely negligent the award would probably be based under the common law. Unfortunately, a more detailed discussion is outside the scope of this book.

Unfair Contract Terms Act (UCTA) 1977 provides:

If a contract contains a term which would exclude or restrict –
a) any liability to which a party to a contract may be subject by reason of any misrepresentation made by him before the contract was made:
    or
b) any remedy available to another party to the contract by reason of such misrepresentation
that term shall be of no effect except in so far as it satisfies the requirements of reasonableness and it is for those claiming that the term satisfies that requirement to show that it does.

Requirement provided by the above Act is that the term shall have been a fair and reasonable one to be included having regard to the circumstances which were, or ought reasonably to have been known to or in the contemplation of the parties, when the contract was made.

In such cases a franchise would be protected as a court would hardly be prepared to hold a term fair and reasonable if it sought to exclude liability for representations made during the negotiation of a franchise.

Equitable relief

It has been argued that the relationship of franchisor–franchisee is a 'fiduciary' relationship. This means that the franchisor should always act in good faith. He should not
* misrepresent or conceal information
* put himself in a position where his duty and interests conflict
He should account for all profits made which arise from the fiduciary relationship. Any secret profits that the franchisor does make in such a way are held on trust for the franchisees. Such a 'constructive' trust will come into being for example:
- where the franchisor has set up a misleading accounting system.
- where a franchisor is withholding supplies from a franchisee.
- where a franchisor is deliberately weakening a franchisee by unfair competition through company-owned outlets.
- where a franchisor is discriminating against particular franchisees.

As has been illustrated above, there are ways that our legal system can deal with franchising problems. However, these tend to be limited and as yet no specific franchise legislation exists. Until full disclosure requirements are obligatory and franchise legislation exists, every franchisee should be aware that only limited protection is available and they should be hyper-cautious before taking out a franchise. They should ensure all details are in writing and they should keep minutes of meetings and telephone calls with their franchisor. All complaints should be in writing and replies carefully kept. Such procedures may seem laborious but are essential should problems arise and solicitors need to be consulted.

Trade Descriptions Act (TDA) 1968

This Act applies to goods and services supplied by:
* franchisor to franchisee under the agreement
* franchisee to customer
The Act deals with goods 'supplied' regardless of being sold, hired or leased. Even if they are 'supplied' free of charge they fall within the ambit of the Act.

Section 1 of the TDA provides that any person who in the course of a trade or business applies a false trade description to any goods, or supplies or offers to supply any goods to which a false description is applied shall be guilty of an offence. Trade description relates inter alia to quantity, size, method of manufacture production, processing, composition, fitness for purpose, testing by any person and the results thereof and approval of any person. Oral statements are sufficient in making a 'trade description'.

False and misleading statements
Section 14 of the TDA states that it is an offence for a person in the
course of any trade or business to 'knowingly' or 'recklessly' make
statements which are false. Therefore, if the franchisor deliberately
makes false or misleading statements on any matter they will fall within
this section, providing the franchisee has not deliberately refrained
from making enquiries.

As discussed earlier, statements such as a 'business of your own' –
'be your own boss' in the franchising context are misleading and
contravene Section 14. Misleading statements as to franchise failure
rates would also probably infringe Section 14. It is arguable academic-
ally that if a statement is made about future services to be provided by
the franchisor himself, such as training and assistance in running the
business, and he has no intention in any real sense of providing those
services, he could be prosecuted under Section 14 and he could also be
guilty of obtaining a pecuniary advantage by deception.

Persistent unfair conduct
Under Part III of the Fair Trading Act 1973 the Director General of
Fair Trading may take action against individual traders or companies
who persist in a course of conduct which is 'unfair' or 'detrimental' to
the interests of *consumers* in the UK. Unfortunately the definition of
'consumer' excludes persons who receive goods or services in the
course of a business and therefore these provisions cannot apply to the
relationship between franchisor and franchisee.

Many professionals feel that the franchisor–franchisee relationship
should be covered under 'consumer' and proposals are being put
forward to create perhaps a quasi-consumer class which will cover the
franchise relationship.

Consumer Credit Act 1974

The Act may apply where the franchisee raises some or all of the
capital to start the business through a loan. If the loan does not exceed
£5,000 the agreement will be a 'consumer credit agreement'. It does not
matter if the loan is to be used for business as long as it is to an
'individual'. Partnerships are included but *not* corporations. A Consumer Credit agreement is a regulated agreement and may be
cancelled within the 'cooling off' period specified by the Act. It is
possible to cancel unless the agreement is secured on land or it is signed
at the business premises of the creditor, owner, party to a linked
transaction or negotiator.

These provisions are very useful for small investors. Antecedent
negotiations are deemed to have been conducted by the negotiator, as
agent for the creditor who is therefore liable for misrepresentations.

Pyramid selling

Where a franchise business is essentially a trade in the sale of franchises, rather than traders in the product of the franchises then the franchisor is pyramid selling and not franchising. The Fair Trading Act 1973 deals with the pyramid selling type of problem and successfully eliminates the worst abusors in this area.

Pyramid selling has been described as follows:

The typical multi-level distributorship plan involves the manufacture or sale by a company under its own trade name of a line of products through 'franchises' which appear to be regular franchise distributorships. These plans may include three to five levels of nonexclusive distributorships and individuals may become franchisees at any level by paying the Company an initial fee based on the level of entry. Once a member of the plan, the individual earns a commission by selling the Company's products and attracting new members. Each distributor pays less for the product than the price he receives from the public and from those at lower levels in the distribution chain to whom he sells. Since one profits merely by being a link in the product distribution chain, the emphasis is on recruiting more investor-distributors rather than on retailing products.

61 Georgetown LJ 1257 1973

Pyramid schemes are financially beneficial for those at the top of the pyramid. Eventually, however, the market will become saturated and recruitment of further participants will not be possible and the whole system will collapse.

Franchises and prospective franchisees should be aware of the above problem and particularly avoid franchises where the franchisor is more interested in attaining a rapid increase in the number of units opening in a given time rather than ensuring that sufficient support is given to existing franchise units.

11
Other sources of information

It is essential for anyone contemplating a franchise opportunity to be aware of all the sources of information which are in fact at their fingertips. It is not suggested that you should rush out and buy the following reports or manuals. Have a look at them at a business library. They will give you a feel for franchising and you will be better equipped for making valid judgments on whether or not you really wish to go into franchising.

The Mintel Report, 1987 Opportunities in Franchising
Mintel Publications Ltd
Kae House, 7 Arundel Street
LONDON WC2R 3DR
Very interesting reading, although probably a bit heavy going in areas. If you cannot manage all of it, read Section one. This deals with current basic market facts, the franchisee-franchisor relationship, financing a franchise and the BFA. Section two deals with the future of franchising. It will give you a general idea of the franchise market.

Keynote Report – Franchising
Keynote Publications Ltd
28–42 Banner Street
LONDON EC1Y 8QE
01–253 3006
Blissfully short – only 36 pages – and to the point! Easy to read. Definitely read all of it.

Euromonitor – Franchising
87–88 Turnmill Street
LONDON EC1M 5QU
The first three sections are general franchising information and are worth reading. Other sections examine particular franchise markets, e.g. 'Franchise Food Retailing'. For those readers who know what market interests them it would be worth reading the relevant section.

Euromonitor – Franchising in the European Economy
Useful if you are planning to go into business abroad or you are
intending to take on a franchise that started abroad.

Business Format Franchising
The Economist Intelligence Unit
40 Duke Street
LONDON W1M 5DG
01–493 6711
General reading on franchising. It is out of date now regarding
specialized information but the general principles are still sound.

Jordan's – UK Franchising – A Financial Survey
Jordan House
Brunswick Place
LONDON N16EE
01–253 3030
Gives a balance sheet and profit and loss account for a number of
franchises and other financial related information.

Franchise Directories and Magazines
Franchise Manual & Directory
Well worth browsing through a copy
of this. Has useful articles worth
reading. Publish *Franchise World*
Magazine which can be subscribed
to.

Bob Riding
James House
37 Nottingham Road
LONDON SW17 7EA
01–767 1371

The Power Report
Franchising: The industry and the Market (Changes in Scale &
Structure – 1984–1986), Michael Power
Power Research Associates
17 Wigmore Street
London
W1H 9LA
01–580 5816
It is a very interesting report containing many useful statistics. The
reader will certainly find it useful and should be able to get a copy from
a business library.

Exhibitions
Potential franchisees should not be in a rush to get into business. They
should take their time and carry out all the research methodically and
meticulously. This process should take at least a year.

   One of the best sources of information are franchise exhibitions.
However, you should note the following points

* Only go to well-known and reputable franchise exhibitions.
* Some exhibitors combine 'business opportunities' with 'franchise opportunities'. This leaves a lot to be desired because you may not know exactly what you are getting into.
* You should *never* sign any contract at an exhibition. If you are interested in something simply make a further appointment.

Regional exhibitions
It is very important that people are made aware of the advantages of franchising. Exhibitors have quite correctly decided to spread the gospel but unfortunately so far the standard of these exhibitions is extremely poor. Why is it poor?
1) The exhibitions are small and unrepresentative of the vast numbers of quality franchises available.
2) They mix business opportunities with franchising.
3) The organizers tend to be in a Catch 22 position – they want to please the paying exhibitor and thereby are prevented from allowing speakers at lectures from saying what needs to be said, i.e. what safeguards should be taken. In such a situation the exhibitors hold the balance of power. They dictate what should be said. Certainly the organizers disapprove of speakers who state hard hitting facts because some of their exhibitors, cannot satisfy the criteria laid down.

No reputable franchisor minds what is said because they abide by the rules, ethics and criteria laid down. The reader should attend a large exhibition where the balance of power problem does not exist. It is recommended that they visit the *National Franchise Exhibition* at Kensington, London which is held every October. Full details can be obtained from the BFA. The exhibition lasts three days and at least a hundred and twenty exhibitors are usually present. About thirteen thousand people visited the exhibition and most attended the lectures and seminars held each day. This year the author will be giving a seminar there. The BFA tries to ensure that unsuitable potential exhibitors are turned away.

As the reader can see, there is a wealth of information on franchising. Choose carefully – there is no need to get swamped by the reports and lose sight of the purpose for reading them. For example, the following method of research would prove invaluable.
1) **Read all of the *Keynote Report*.**
2) **Read one of the other reports for more detail – only the relevant parts.**
3) **Have a quick look at the *Power Report* in the library.**
4) **Read the Franchise Manual 7 Directory (from *Franchise World*), paying particular attention to the articles.**

5) Obtain the BFA 'A Comprehensive Guide to Franchising' package and read cover to cover.
6) Attend the Kensington Franchise Exhibition.

12

The future of franchising – Growth and new developments

In this chapter the growth of franchising both in the UK and Europe, together with a look at a couple of variations on the franchising scene which have appeared in Europe and which we may see here in the UK in the near future will be discussed. Deterrants to the growth of franchising, and what can be learned from the experiences of two particular franchises, namely, La Mama, and Holland & Barratt will be considered. Finally a look at Wimpy and Tie Rack, two successful franchisors, to see what can be learnt from their development and policies and what a franchisee needs to look out for to identify a successful franchise.

Franchising is certainly here to stay. It is a superb way of carrying on a business providing it is done correctly and ethically. Those of us involved in the franchising industry must ensure that potential franchisees are well informed and that the franchisors adhere to the highest standards. A number of franchisors entering the market during the sixties and seventies are still expanding and trading successfully today. Many successful and respectable franchising companies do exist. Unfortunately franchising still has to live down the reputation it inherits from those who exploit the concept. The only way to avoid this would appear to be tighter controls and this will be reviewed later.

The present UK market

At the moment the large established companies are continuing to expand but very slowly. There are many new entrants and these are growing and consolidating their position and trying to achieve their sales targets. The question that arises is 'What is going to happen in the next few years?' Well, there are two possibilities; either the new companies will achieve their objectives leading to great growth or there may be many failures. Who can tell? Providing growth is cautious and the new franchisors do their homework there is every chance of continued growth. Existing established franchisors should be planning to adapt to the changes in the market and environment. They must ensure that they keep up-to-date with new market trends, renew their know-how and be prepared to change products if necessary.

In their recent survey Power Research Associates estimated that there are 440 franchise systems in operation (270 of them being involved in business format franchising). There are about 19,800 actual units in existence with average annual sales of £113,000. Total sales are now in the region of £2.2 billion and the total number of individuals working for franchises is 149,000 (including franchisees and those employed at franchise units and headquarters). They predict that by 1991 there will be £6.1 billion sales generated by a 140 per cent increase in existing systems (allowing 16 per cent for closures).

The *Power Report* establishes the five largest areas of franchising as being:
* home improvement and maintenance
* leisure products and services
* fast food restaurants
* clothing and fashion
* professional and commercial services to business

It predicts that the greatest expansion will be in leisure products and services, mobile food and drink, and business property maintenance; the least expansion in clothing and fashion, transport of parcels and goods and fast food retailing.

Certainly there seems to be a lot of scope for expansion when you consider that in France, which has a similar population to the UK, franchise sales are three times the UK level.

The *Power Report* goes on to consider the relations between franchisor and franchisee and comes up with '9 strands' in this relationship:
1) Support from the franchisor.
2) Confidence in the franchisor's ability.
3) Confidence in the franchisor's motivation.
4) Pressure exerted by the franchisor.
5) Scope for consultation and communication.
6) Realization of mutual interest.
7) Personal rapport.
8) Market potential.
9) Terms and agreements.

Clearly these are all essential ingredients in the make-up of a franchise that is going to be successful. Franchisees and franchisors need to be aware of these '9 strands' and ensure that throughout the life of a franchise system standards are maintained which keep the score high on each issue.

The *Power Report* came up with five principal difficulties experienced by franchisees. In descending order of importance these are:

1) Competition
2) Finding staff
3) Financial planning and cash flow
4) Low sales
5) Margins/terms/discounts.

The conclusion the report reached was that while franchisors were providing the franchisee with a name, a method, location and even in some cases finance they did not find them customers at the end of the day or show them how to win over competitors.

It is clear that franchisors need to concentrate more on providing franchisees with adequate training which requires a commitment by the franchisor of sufficient resources to provide both initial and on-going training. From the franchisees' point of view, it is essential that they are satisfied from the outset that they will be provided with adequate initial training and just as importantly on-going training throughout the period of the franchise contract.

This is supported by Tony Dutfield of the BFA who stresses that in a number of cases franchisee training was quite inadequate. While leading franchisors like MacDonalds with their 'Hamburger University' and Tie Rack with their 'Tie Rack School' can devote sufficient resources to provide adequate training to franchisees, many other franchisors just do not devote sufficient resources or commitment to a training programme. Regrettably this is too often the case with new franchise concepts.

Hence, the BFA will in the future be providing special 'franchising training' sessions which franchisors will be able to use (and pay for) to ensure that franchisees really know what is going on and can manage their business. The training is to consist of everything from filling in an employee returns form to 'how to sell'.

Expansion from the UK
As plans such as the one above come into being they will inevitably lead to more confidence in the franchising industry and in turn aid expansion. Already there has been expansion from the UK market into Europe (particularly France and Germany) by a number of established franchisors, for example, Wimpy and the Body Shop.

Expansion from the USA into the UK
More apparent to the reader will be the expansion into the UK from the USA market. Certainly, this will continue, particularly in the fields of fast food, restaurants and computer franchises. The USA market is wider and stronger than ours and new ideas can be tested easily there. However, this situation must be treated with caution – the USA market is very different to the UK market and, where a US franchise is brought to the UK, there have been a number of franchises which have suffered because insufficient market research of the UK market was carried out in the first instance.

A prime example of the market differences is 'fast food'. The British are not as addicted to hamburgers as some franchisors would like. The only way forward in this case is slow cautious expansion.

The European market

It is forecast that business format franchise sales in Western Europe will nearly double from US $25.87 billion in 1986 to US $49.60 billion in 1990; the number of active franchisors will increase from 2,197 in 1986 to 3,550 in 1990; the number of franchisees will increase from 89,805 in 1986 to 155,500 in 1990. These figures are obtained from the Euromonitor report and are illustrated in the following tables:

Table 12.1   Forecast Franchisee Numbers By Country 1986–1990

	1986e	1987f	1988f	1990f
Belgium	3,600	4,200	4,500	5,000
France	24,000	30,000	38,000	41,000
Italy	5,500	7,600	9,000	12,000
Netherlands	7,200	7,800	8,500	10,000
Portugal	500	620	1,100	1,500
Sweden	2,205	2,600	3,000	4,000
United Kingdom	19,800	26,000	30,000	40,000
West Germany	20,000	22,000	26,000	30,000
Denmark, Spain, Norway, Greece	7,000	8,500	10,000	12,000
TOTAL	89,805	109,320	130,100	155,500

Source: Euromonitor

Table 12.2   Forecast Franchisee Sales By Country 1986–1990

$ billion, constant 1986	1986e	1987f	1988f	1990f
Belgium	2.10	2.30	3.00	3.60
France	10.00	12.00	15.50	18.00
Italy	2.30	3.00	3.80	5.00
Netherlands	5.40	6.60	7.00	9.00
Portugal	0.20	0.28	0.39	0.60
Sweden	0.70	0.86	1.00	1.50
United Kingdom	2.60	3.60	5.00	7.00
West Germany	1.70	2.20	2.80	3.30
Denmark, Spain, Norway, Greece	0.87	1.06	1.30	1.60
TOTAL	25.87	31.90	39.79	49.60

Source: Euromonitor

Table 12.3   Forecast Franchisor Numbers By Country 1986–1990

	1986e	1987f	1988f	1990f
Belgium	100	120	135	160
France	490	550	680	750
Italy	66	83	99	120
Netherlands	236	300	390	430
Portugal	35	60	100	120
Sweden	70	88	110	150
United Kingdom	440	475	520	600
West Germany	320	360	400	500
Denmark, Spain, Norway, Greece	440	580	675	720
TOTAL	2,197	2,616	3,109	3,550

Source: Euromonitor

Table 12.4   Business format franchising in the European economy (reproduced by kind permission of the European Franchising Federation)

1986

Countries	Number of franchisors	%	Number of franchised outlets	%	Sales franchisees in billion ECU	%
1. Belgium	69	4.4	2,744	3.2	2.8	7.5
2. France	456	28.9	22,068	25.4	14.5	39.0
3. Italy (1)	79	4.9	8,024	9.2	2.1	6.2
4. The Netherlands	227	14.4	7,422	8.5	4.8	12.9
5. Spain (1985)	90	5.7	8,200	9.4	1.8	4.9
6. United Kingdom (3)	300	19.0	20,000	23.0	3.2	8.6
7. West Germany (1)	259	16.4	18,000	20.7	7.0	18.9
8. Norway (1985) (2)	65	4.1	–	–	0.6	1.6
9. Sweden	35	2.2	586	0.7	0.3	0.8
Sumtotals	1,580	100.0	87.044 (2)	100.0	37.1	100.0

Sales of Automobiles, Trucks, Petrol, Softdrink bottlers and hotels excluded.
  (1) 1983 estimation
  (2) Number of outlets of Norway not communicated.
  (3) Exclusively Business Format Franchises.
Copyright © Belgium, European Franchising Federation.

The figures for the European community are also of interest. These are illustrated in table 12.4 and reproduced by kind permission of the European Franchising Federation.

Franchising is no longer just a national business. It is now international and will continue to gain momentum as people become more aware of its respectability. The greatest growth is expected in Italy, the UK and Sweden. Mature franchise markets already exist in France, Belgium and the Netherlands.

Franchising variations

Interesting variations on business format franchising have appeared throughout Europe – one such variation is called 'frinchising' and is being developed in the Netherlands on the fringe of the established franchising scene. Basically it has developed because large Dutch symbol retailers have tried to gain control over shops by converting them into franchises. Needless to say, the independent retailers using their symbol have resisted and the symbol retailers have adopted the word 'frinchising' to cover their method of operation which does in fact give more independence than a traditional business format franchise.

Gerant libre – 'the quasi-franchise'
This is another variation on the franchising theme which has come into being particularly in France. It is rather like the tied tenancy – public house agreements in the UK.

Basically, the company or 'quasi-franchisor' provides the business premises, the name, goodwill etc., as in a franchise, and the 'quasi franchisee' i.e. the *gerant libre* buys the stock and employs his own staff and pays the rent and so on. The business profits are shared in an agreed ratio – usually one third to the *gerant libre* and two thirds to the company, but of course the parties involved can agree to any ratio. The advantage to the company or quasi franchisor is that he has in effect a highly motivated manager working in the business which will reflect profitability. The advantage to the *gerant libre* is that he has a stake in the business and enjoys a certain amount of freedom.

Operations such as these will become more common in the future and certainly something to look out for.

Deterrents to the growth in the UK market

Even though there is no doubt that franchising will continue to grow the rate at which this growth will proceed depends on a number of factors.

Scandal

Franchising has proved its respectability in many cases, but there is still a lingering doubt in many people's minds when they hear scandal. Over the last few years there has been a wave of 'franchise failure' stories in the newspapers; a few years before that there were nothing but good stories. Suddenly, after the collapse of the Young's Group and, in particular, 'La Mama' which sold maternity wear, the whole issue of franchising came under close scrutiny and critical comment. Indeed, overnight it became fashionable to talk of franchise failures.

The Young's group – Pronuptia, Young's Formal Menswear, La Mama

The Young's Group went into receivership in November 1985. Prior to that date the group, which included Pronuptia (wedding dresses), Young's Formal Menswear and La Mama (maternity wear), was a full member of the BFA even though in the case of La Mama in reality it had failed to meet the BFA's criteria for membership. The management of the Young's group and everybody associated with it appeared to have satisfactory franchising credentials. A major institution, the National Coal Board Pension Fund, had even made a substantial investment in the group.

In late 1985 the group's bankers, Barclays Bank, appointed a receiver and certain members of the senior management moved abroad. The group was acquired by Cyril Spencer, formerly a director of Burton's and Chairman of Waring and Gillow plc.

For many months prior to the receivership, because of the cash flow difficulties of the group, franchisees experienced increasing difficulty in obtaining stock, which had an immediate and adverse effect on their business. Advertising and publicity, which the franchisor was contractually obliged to provide, deteriorated. For reasons outside the control of each franchisee their franchisor's own financial and managerial weaknesses were adversely affecting their businesses. The franchise umbrella was leaking, and subsequently collapsed.

For La Mama franchisees the new management under Cyril Spencer failed to fulfil their initial promises that La Mama would be developed and more resources committed to it. Despite repeated statements of support to the La Mama concept made by the management, within a year a chain of over twenty franchise and company shops had ceased trading as a chain. Belatedly, the management declared the chain non-viable while they concentrated their resources on developing the Pronuptia and Young's Formal Menswear chains.

For those La Mama franchisees who had to cease trading substantial personal losses were inevitable. For selected franchisees the company offered settlements while others were not offered any settlement. Some franchisees were left owing their bankers significant debts. At least one franchisee commenced legal proceedings against the company.

A combination of receivership together with a lack of commitment by the new management proved disastrous for the La Mama concept and its franchisees – having been a franchisee of La Mama at the time of the collapse, I can assure the reader that such problems only arise when a franchise is not operated correctly. La Mama was a regrettable example of what can go wrong and how it is the franchisees who suffer most for the shortfalls and failures of the franchisor's management. The failure of La Mama, however, cannot be laid at the door of franchising. A franchise is only as good as its management and the concept it offers. Franchising CAN and DOES work.

The La Mama problems lay in the following areas:
 1) Insufficient market research into the market for maternity wear in this country.
 2) Inadequate pilot operations.
 3) Poor site selection.
 4) Poor quality control of goods.
 5) Non-competitive prices.
 6) Poor communications.
 7) Over optimistic sales projections.
 8) Poor back-up services.
 9) Poor merchandising.
10) Poor training of franchisees in sales.
11) Poor company management.

I am always asked whether the above experience has made me view franchising in a bad light – I would say, once and for all NO!! I believe in the concept of franchising and know that it can work. There is absolutely no sense in viewing things bitterly. One must learn from experience. And if one can help others learn from that experience so much the better.

There are many good things that came out of the La Mama experience, namely:
1) An awareness that franchising, like all businesses, does carry a risk even though that risk is considerably reduced.
2) The importance of research of the franchise opportunity.
3) The importance of market research.
4) Tighter controls imposed by the BFA.
5) An awareness by the BFA that franchisees need good training facilities which are not always provided.
6) An awareness by the BFA that a 'concilation service' – arbitration service (as explained in Chapter 4) would be very useful for franchisees who often cannot afford to go to court.
7) A need for 'educating' potential franchisees as to exactly what they are going into.
8) A need to highlight any problems in any given area.

None of us dedicated to franchising want to see scandal. We have no time for the cowboys in the business who want to make a fast buck. What we do want to do is to help franchisees to succeed.

The way it should be done – Holland & Barrett
In complete contrast to the debacle of La Mama would appear to be Holland & Barrett Health Food Stores, which started out in 1970 and started franchising in 1982 when they already had about 150 of their own company shops. They now have a total of about 230 shops throughout the UK, including 23 franchised units. Holland & Barrett have decided to stop franchising. Over the next few years they will be buying back the franchised shops at market value.
*   Why has franchising not worked for them? What problems did they experience?
*   What can we learn from their experiences?

Problems
1) Firstly it would appear that their major problem was the fast moving market place. So many inroads have been made into health products by big supermarkets such as Sainsbury's that in order to keep a competitive edge they have to adapt changes very quickly. With franchised shops there are two problems:
*   The changes cannot take place as quickly as necessary because the franchisees have to be consulted and allowed time to make a decision.
*   The 'changes' (e.g. refurbishment to change the image of the stores) cost money which a franchisee does not have or cannot raise. Holland & Barrett research shows that they need to refurbish every five years.

So a situation arises where some or all franchisees decide to leave their shops as they are because they cannot afford anything else whilst others and the company shops do adapt to the changes and refurbish. The result is that in time there will no longer be a common corporate image – the very essence of franchising and so some franchisees lag behind. This problem has been experienced by other franchisors such as Kentucky Fried Chicken and Wimpy.

2) The second problem related to the customer's perception of their product mix. Customers are not aware of the difference between health foods and healthy foods. Holland & Barrett deal with the former while supermarkets sell the latter. Their mix of products at the moment is 60 per cent food and 40 per cent non-foods, e.g. vitamins, books, herbal remedies. They have to change this in the future to 60 per cent non-foods, incorporating products for a healthy environment as well as a healthy body, e.g., air purifiers, ionizers, etc. – products which a supermarket is unlikely ever to stock.

3) Originally when Holland & Barrett decided to franchise their

research showed that by employing franchisees who would be more motivated they would achieve higher sales to the tune of at least 10 per cent. In effect, sales increased only by a factor of about 5 per cent. (This could be because the premises had just been refurbished and not because franchisees had started running them.)

4) The cost of franchise support was greater than they had anticipated.

5) The management structure was 'split' and caused great problems because buyers and marketing could not make essential snap decisions. Everything had to be agreed with franchisees which took time.

6) Franchisee selection: they scrutinized their franchisees over a three day period, putting them through many tests and all in all were happy with the franchisees they had taken on. However, they felt that the franchise relationship was such that a franchisee was happy to pay royalties in the early days while they needed much support but became resentful later in the day when they had 'learned' the business. It was a very difficult task to choose franchisees who would remain happy. A balance had to be struck between the complete entrepreneur and someone who would become dissatisfied and demotivated operating within the strict parameters of a franchise. Indeed Holland & Barrett felt that franchisees should be told right at the beginning what a franchise relationship is in no uncertain terms and under no circumstances should they ever be told that they are their own boss – they are not!

7) British personality – Holland & Barrett felt that franchisees needed to be made more aware of the 'profit motive'. Something the Americans are very good at while the British are not.

What lessons can be learnt?
For the franchisor the following are essential:

1) **Ensure that growth by franchising is really what you want/need.**
2) **Rigid selection of franchisees is crucial.**
3) **Adequate market research is essential.**
4) **If anything, overestimate the resources necessary for franchise support.**
5) **It is not a 'make your money quick and run' business. People's livelihoods are at stake.**

For the franchisee the following are essential:

1) **Self-analysis. Can you 'stay alive' within the confines of a franchise, i.e. do you have franchise mentality? If you are too much of an entrepreneur – stay clear – do it yourself!**
2) **Remember you are not your own boss and never will be. Franchising is a halfway house. At best you will be a 'soft entrepreneur'.**
3) **Carry out *all* the research mentioned before.**
4) **Make sure there is adequate initial and ongoing training.**

Generally, Holland & Barrett confirmed that in their view the growth of the UK franchise industry would continue. Franchising could be a profitable method of operation, but they considered the franchising industry needed tighter controls to ensure that the 'cowboy' element was eliminated.

In their own case, where their franchise operation was part of a much larger chain of company-owned retail outlets, franchising did not prove to be the most suitable method of operation. However, because of their resources and managerial commitment to safeguarding the interests of their franchisees, they have implemented a policy of buying back the franchise operations, so that the franchisees avoid significant losses; franchisees who are trading profitably will receive a price that reflects the value of the business.

In summary, Holland & Barrett's advice to would-be franchisees is to exercise caution at all times and to deal only with reputable franchises who have adequate resources to service a franchise network.

Apart from the lingering doubts in people's minds there are other deterrents to the growth of franchising in the UK market, for instance, the **1950 Shops Act**, which restricts Sunday trading and has already affected convenience stores. In some cases Franchisees have had to stop Sunday trading and thereby have not been able to achieve their sales projections; the business has become non-viable and they have had to close down. It is very important to know exactly what opening times the projections are based on. Remember, you may not be able to trade on Sunday, and if the projections have been based on Sunday opening then they are useless.

Legislation and Disclosure

At the present moment there is no franchise legislation and no disclosure requirements – *caveat emptor* '(Let the buyer beware') rules. However, an increasing number of professionals feel that legislation or at least disclosure is necessary for protection of franchisees (and franchisors!).

Others categorically state that legislation will not work and will only serve as a deterrent to franchising growth. Certainly it may do this as franchisors will have to satisfy given criteria which they may not be able to do unless they have traded for a specific time. On the other hand, the USA has franchise legislation and there the franchise industry is flourishing. This is an idea that needs considerable research.

In a recent interview with Tony Dutfield of the BFA on the question of legislation and tighter controls he agreed that this area needed research and that if the case *against* legislation was proven there was still room for other controls to be imposed. For example, the BFA has a problem in that only some franchisors are members. Therefore they can only be a watchdog for these. There is no watchdog for the others, so who controls them? The answer is that nobody has control. The BFA does not have the power to enforce the decisions it makes. It has tried to maximize membership and needs support from all franchisors, not just its members, if its objectives are to be achieved. Tony Dutfield recently commented: 'The successful application of Business Format Franchising requires total acceptance of the BFA code of ethics. We believe that such acceptance will ensure that the dramatic growth of franchising within the UK Market Place predicted by the BFA/Nat West Bank Research of 1987 will be achieved.'

A number of things need to be reviewed within the franchise industry – one of them is whether compulsory registration of a trade association would be beneficial. Another is whether there should be disclosure of certain requirements as a matter of law. It would be useful to have a committee made up of varying backgrounds (and consisting of members and non-members of the BFA) to discuss such issues.

It is always easy to lay down standards. The problem is keeping to them yourself and making sure everybody else adheres to them as well.

When there are controls and standard contracts for purchasers buying a property (National Conditions of Sale, or Law Society Conditions) surely there is a need to look at what controls are necessary for purchasers of franchises. The decision to invest in a particular business is as important and crucial as the decision to buy a particular house. Disclosure would be like a survey, i.e. not a 100 per cent guarantee that everything is satisfactory but an indication of things to be aware of and to watch out for.

It proved to be well worth asking a couple of prominent franchisors in the UK what they thought of the future of franchising and to what they attributed their success and what a franchisee should look out for.

The success of Wimpy

Fast food in the UK, including take-away restaurants, adds up to a turnover of about £1,300 million per annum. That market is roughly divided up as follows:

Fish & Chips	45%
Hamburgers	30%
Chicken	10%
Pizza	10%
Miscellaneous (Indian, Chinese etc.)	5%
	100%

Wimpy has over 100 restaurants which are counter service in style. They began trading over thirty years ago. In 1976 they were bought by United Biscuits. Under the parent company's long-term investment programme they introduced counter service and pursued a policy of upgrading product quality and greater product diversification. Today they serve over 80 million customers annually throughout the Wimpy franchise. In the UK alone it has a turnover of well over £100 million (company and franchised units). Wimpy directly employ 2,000 people, but some 9,000 to 10,000 people actually depend on Wimpy for their livelihood through the franchise network.

Wimpy International is totally committed to franchising. About twenty restaurants are retained as company-owned and are used to test new products and designs. Wimpy attributes its success to quality of product and proportion, choosing and developing the right franchisee and finding the right site.

The future in franchising

Wimpy believes that the retail and service industry climate is such that franchising will develop at a much greater rate than ever before. They feel that as the climate becomes more conducive to owning one's own business, and as the entrepreneurial culture develops, so expansion of the market will speed up. They are open to developing new concepts, for example Drive-Thru restaurants, to keep up with market changes.

Franchise legislation

Wimpy International is a founder member of the BFA. It does, however, believe that firm policing is necessary if additional legislation is to be avoided.

From a Franchisee's Point of View

They think it is essential that a franchisee looks for a good track record in order to reassure himself that the services and support provided by the franchisor are substantial enough to warrant payments.

Concerning franchisee selection, they state that they look for energy, enthusiasm, business experience and a mutual trust in the franchise business.

What makes Tie Rack tick?

Tie Rack had a number of small shops before they started to franchise. They found the shops were making money but they had a staff problem. They wanted to expand. Roy Bishko had problems envisaging how to run a chain of 100 shops when they had problems running 10 – his answer was franchising.

He was and is a keen follower of McDonald's and was fascinated by their 'Q.S.V.' (quality, service and value) standard. If McDonald's were prepared to give a share of the profits of their successful shops in return for dedicated people managing outlets so could he. In order to attain the common denominator of uniformity, attention to detail, service and quality Tie Rack developed a method of operation by which they maintain considerable control. Tie Rack take a lease on the premises, design and fit the unit and then either sublet or license the completed unit to a franchisee. Tie Rack pays all the rent, rates and service charges. The franchisee pays a turnover related fee.

Tie Rack benefits from growth in franchisee sales and the franchisee benefits by having a prime retail site that only Tie Rack with its financial muscle could obtain.

Bishko stresses the importance of ploughing back money into the infrastructure of the business system, and the fact that they started franchising what were already successful businesses. He has a total commitment to franchising and the involvement of franchisees which he thinks is essential to a system that will stand the test of time. He states:

We have avoided charging large upfront fees. Such large initial charges should be regarded as a possible danger sign that a potential franchisee should look out for. Our policy is rather to participate in the profits and growth of each franchised business as it develops so that together with the franchisee we build up the Business.

Modelled on McDonald's University of Hamburgerology, he has founded his own Tie Rack School of Ties which provides training courses for staff and franchisees. He is committed to intensive initial and continual training.

Tie Rack is a member of the BFA because they feel that regulation of franchising is necessary. Bishko notes that the BFA has no legal authority and states that for that reason membership of the BFA should not be regarded as an endorsement, but that non-membership should be regarded as a possible danger sign. It is worth noting, however, that neither McDonald's nor the Body Shop, both very successful format franchisors, are BFA members.

Conclusion

The essential ingredients for a successful franchise (whatever it is) are the same. Whether the franchisor has decided eventually to give up franchising or is successfully franchising they all stipulate the need for six success factors:
1) **Excellent market research.**
2) **Excellent training.**
3) **Good locations.**

4) **Strong control over franchisees.**
5) **Strong management team totally committed to franchising.**
6) **A foundation of a successful business which is proven.**

One franchisor stated that there are only two real reasons why a company would want to franchise:

1) To use franchisee financial resources to expand.
2) To have committed and motivated individuals running their businesses.

With regard to the second point, Tie Rack is a prime example of using committed individuals for already successful businesses.

The problems arise when the system has not really been proven. The would-be franchisor thinks it will work because his one or two shops work, and he has not the resources to expand further. He then thinks he will expand by using franchising and other people's money. But the problem is that he has not the resources to carry out the market research or give adequate training or obtain prime locations, and does not have the strong management team to support the franchisees. This type of franchisor is potentially very dangerous. If the business works – fine! If it doesn't then the franchisor will not be in a position to assist franchisees or bail them out. Thus, franchisees should be particularly careful in such cases.

The same franchisor stated that there are a number of cowboys in the business and the franchisee should be warned of this. Some cowboys use the BFA as a cloak of respectability – until there are legal controls franchisees should be warned of this as well.

It would appear from all the research that franchisees should:

1) **Be cautious.**
2) **Carry out all the research stipulated.**
3) **Ensure that the '6 success factors' are present in the franchise they are considering investing in.**
4) **Have faith in the franchise concept because it does work.**

Franchisees should only invest in businesses that have proven themselves successful and then invest with confidence and be prepared to work hard and with two things always in mind:

* The profit motive.
* Faith in the franchising relationship which gave them the opportunity to run their own business – an opportunity which they may not otherwise have had.

The author hopes that she has been successful in highlighting all the good and problematic areas in franchising so as to enable the reader to make an informed decision on one of the most important things in his or her life.

Only one thing remains to be said – Good luck!

Appendices

Summary of franchise listing

(Reproduced by kind permission of *Franchise World*. Detailed listing available from *Franchise World Directory*)

Name	Type of Business	Investment Cost excluding Working Capital	Address
Accounting Centre	Accounting Services	£7,500	El Scott House Arcadia Avenue N3 2JE 01–349 3191
Alan Paul	Hairdressing	£25,000–£45,000	164 New Chester Road Birkenhead Merseyside 051 660 1060
Alfred Marks	Employment Bureau		Adia House 84–86 Regent Street London W1A 1AL 01–437 7855
Alpine Soft Drinks	Home deliveries of soft drinks		Richmond Way Chelmsley Wood Birmingham 021 770 6816
Amtrak Express Parcels	Parcel deliveries	£8,500–£15,000	Company House Tower Hill Bristol B52 0EQ
ANC Parcel Service	Parcel deliveries		Berryhill Victoria Road Fenton Stoke on Trent 0782 260478

Anicare Veterinary Group	Vet practice	£5,000	23 Buckingham Road Shoreham-by-Sea W. Sussex 0273 463022
Ap Autela	Motor component distributor	£44,000	PO Box 80 Tachbrook Road Leamington Spa Warcs CV31 3QR 0926 883621
Apollo Window Blinds	Manuf/retail of window blinds	£22,000	Johnstone Avenue Glasgow GS2 4YH 041 810 3021
Athena	Retailing posters	£65,000	Pentos Retailing Corp Ltd Berwick House Livery Street Birmingham 021 236 6886
Applied Motors	Distribution/replacement parts of VW/Audi vehicles		Victoria Wharf Dragoon Road London SE8 3NW 01–691 5921
Atlantis Watersports	Water sports and diving equipment	£40,000–£60,000	97 Saltergate Chesterfield 0709 371 977
Autosheen	Mobile car valeting	£4,950	37 Billing Road Northampton 0604 232244
Avis	Short term vehicle hire	£25,000	Trident House Station Road Hayes, UB3 4DJ 01–848 8765
A1 Damproofing	Damp treatment and timber preservation	£11,000	New Side Mill Charnley Fold Lane Bamber Bridge Preston 0772 35228
Badgeman	Badge printing and enparring	£20,000	Sketchley Bus. Service Grp. Rugby Road Hinckley Leics LE10 2NE 0455 38133

Bally	Shoe retailing	£120,000	Wells House 79 Wells Street London W1P 4JL 01–631 4222
Balmforth & Partners	Estate agency	£18,000–£22,000	St Marys House Duke Street Norwich 0603 660555
Baraman	Promotional items	£37,225	78 Newman Street London W1 01–636 7777
Banson Tool Hire	Hire and sale of tools	£40,000	Pellon Lane Halifax West Yorks 0422 50617
Baskin Robbins	Ice cream parlours	from £25,000	Glacier House Oldfield Lane Greenford, Middx 01–575 2004
Bath Doctor	Bathroom renovation	£5,000–£11,000	Denbigh House Denbigh Road Milton Keynes 0908 270007
Bath Wizard	Re-surfacing bathroom suites	£10,000	Bath Trans- formations Ltd Victory Business Centre Somers Road North Portsmouth 0705 753719
Bella Pizza	Home delivery and take away pizzas	£70,000	8 Cowgate Peterborough PE1 0733 49797
Bellina	Retail of Belgian chocolates	£20,000	Bellina Ltd Penny Corner Farthing Road Sproughton Indus. Estate, Ipswich 0473 40275
Berni	Restaurant	£275,000	Grand Metropolitan Retailing Limited 106 Oxford Road Uxbridge, Middx 0895 70955

Body Reform	Retail of natural toiletries and beauty products	£35,000	Natural Beauty Products Ltd Unit 5 Kingsway Buildings Bridgend Industrial Estate Bridgend Mid-Glamorgan 0656 5710114
Body Shop (The)	Retail of natural skin and hair products	£140,000	Hawthorn Road Wick Littlehampton West Sussex 0903 717107
Brick-tie services	Replacement of corroded wall tiles	£9,810	Yorkshire House Easy Road Leeds West Yorks 0532 487387
Brittania Business Sales	Licensed trade specialists	£17,000	Skyline Chambers 14 Manor Row Bradford West Yorkshire 0274 722 977
British Damp Proofing	Damp control and timber preservation	£10,500	The Old School House Fleetwood Road Esprick Preston PR4 3HJ 039 136 441
Budget Rent-a-car	Car/van/truck rental	£75,000	41 Marlowes Hemel Hempstead Herts HP1 1LD 0442 232555
Burger King	Hamburger restaurant	£500,000–£600,000	20 Kew Road Richmond Surrey 01–940 6046
Captain Cargo	Next day freight delivery and collection	£7,500	Wetherby Road Ascot Drive Indust. Estate Derby 0332 290810

Caroll	Fashion retailers	£25,000–£50,000	Caroll Carlon Ltd 68–70 Kings Road London SW3 01–581 0304
Castle Fairs	Exhibition organisers	£7,500	Bowcliffe Road Bramham Wetherby Yorkshire 0937 845 829
Chemical Express	Mobile showroom supplying repeat order products to industry	£6,900	Chemical Express Group Ninian Way Wilnecote Tamworth, Staffs 0827 251 431
Chicken George	Chicken take-away/ restaurant	£44,000	Shirley Lodge 470 London Road Slough 0753 684 926
CICO	Renovation and lining of old and new chimneys	£14,000	Westleton Saxmundham Suffolk 072 873 608
Circle C	Convenience stores	£70,000–£90,000	24 Fitzalan Road Roffey Horsham West Sussex 0403 210450
City Link	Parcel collection and delivery service	£25,000	Bataria Road Sunbury-on-Thames Middx TW6 5LR 0932 788799
Clarks	Shoe retailers	£75,000	Torlink Ltd Box 106 40 High Street Somerset BA16 0YA 0458 43131
Clean Machine	Mobile car valeting		5 Herbrand Street London WC1 278 3101
Coca-Cola	Soft drinks		Pemberton House Wrights Lane London W8 01–938 2131

Coffeeman	Retail of fresh ground coffee	£8,000	73 Woolsbridge Industrial Park Wimborne, Dorset 0202 823501
Colour Counsellors	Interior decorating advisory service		187 New Kings Rd Parsons Green London SW6 01–736 8326
Command Performance	Hairdressing	£50,000	High End Troutstream Way Loudwater WD3 4LQ 0923 777636
Complete Cookshop	Gifts & house wares retailers	£60,000	Enterprise House Buckingham Road Aylesbury, Bucks 0296 431 296
Complete Engraver & Colourist	Glass engraving	£12,575	T C Graphics Ltd Valley House Needham Harleston, Norfolk 0379 852168
Computa Tune	Mobile car tuning and servicing	£9,500	Unit 3 Richmond Industrial Estate Brown Street Accrington, Lancs 0254 385891/ 391792
Complete Weed Control	Amenity and industrial weed control	£12,000	Langstone Priory Mews Station Road Kingham, Oxon 060 871 8851
Computerland	Retailers of computer hardware & software	£400,000	518 Elder House Eldergate Central Milton Keynes 0908 664244
Cornerstone (WC £25,000)	Estate agency		Abbey National Estate Agency Limited Abbey House Baker Street London NW1 01–486 5555

Country Properties	Estate agency		6c Brand Street Hitchin SG5 1HX 0462 54040
Countrywide Garden Maintenance Services	Garden maintenance on fixed yearly contract		164–200 Stockport Road Cheadle, Cheshire 061 428 4444
Creteprint paving	Coloured paving systems	£20,000	Cobblestone Paving Ltd Unit 12, Wheatear Perry Road Whitham, Essex 0376 517766
Crimecure/30	Installation of security systems	£7,500	Darley House Cow Lane Garston Watford, Herts 0923 663322
Crown Eyegloss Optical Centre	Spectacle retailers	£9,000	Stancliffe Street Blackburn, Lancs 0254 51535
Curtain Dream	Retailer of soft funishings	£20,000	63 Nesfield Street Bradford West Yorks 0274 728719
Dampco	Rising damp and wood preservation	£10,500	21 Lytham Lane Coventry 0203 687683
Dampcure- Woodcure/30	Damp & timber treatments	£9,000	Darley House Cow Lane Garston, Watford Herts 0923 66322
Damptechnik	Damp & timber treatments	£10,750	Damptechnik House George Street Mandale Triangle Thornaby Cleveland 0642 606484/ 670666
Dash	Fashion retailer		PO Box 5 Rowdell Road Northolt, Middx 01–845 7777

Direct Salon Services	Sale of hairdressing products to saloons		Newport Way Camon Park Middlesborough Cleveland 0642 217978
Domino's Pizza	Pizza restaurant & take away		Blue Companies Ltd Beck Row Mildenhall Suffolk 0638 716711
Don Millers Hot Bread Kitchens	Hot bread kitchens	£90,000–£110,000	166 Bute Street Mall Arndale Centre Luton LU1 2TL 0582 422 781
Dyno-Electrics	Electrical contracting	£1,650	Dyno Rod Developments 143 Maple Road Surbiton KT6 4JB 01–549 9711
Dyno-Rod	Maintenance and cleaning of drains, pipes & sewers	variable according to size of area purchased	143 Maple Road Surbiton KT6 4BJ 01–549 9711
English Rose	Retailing of kitchens	£32,000–£35,000	Ideal Timber Products Ltd Broadmeadow Industrial Estate Dumbarton, Glasgow 0398 61777
Euroclean	Dry cleaning	£62,000	EDS Dry Cleaning Systems Ltd 15 The Mall Heathway Dagenham, Essex 595 4234
Everett Masson & Furby	Business transfer agents	£25,000	18 Walsworth Rd Hitchin SG4 9SP 0462 32377
Eversheds Super Spa	Convenience stores	£65,000–£130,000	PO Box 175 Dolphin Road Shoreham-by-Sea West Sussex 0273 455555

Exchange Travel	Retail travel agency	£30,000	Exchange House Parker Road Hastings, E Sussex TN34 3UB 0424 423571
Fastframe Instant Picture Framing	Picture framing	£34,000	28 Blandford St, Sunderland SR1 3JH 091 5652233
Fatso's Pasta Joint	Pasta restaurant	£80,000	3 Palace Gate Parade Hampton Court East Molesey Surrey 01–783 1664
Fersina	UPVC windows and conservatories	£25,000	Cestrum House Industry Road Carlton Industrial Estate Carlton, Barnsley South Yorks 0226 728310
Flash Trash	Retailer of fashion accessories	£48,500	269 Regent Street London W1 01–491 4251
Foto Inn	1hr film processing		12 Oxford Street London W1N 01–589 0434
Fotofast	Film processing		4th floor Carolyn House 22–26 Dingwall Road Croydon CR0 9XF 01–688 2770
Frame Factory (The)	Framing service	£33,000	67 Vivian Avenue Hendon NW4 01–202 1235
Freezavan	Sale and distribution of frozen food	£5,000	Fleet, Spalding Lincs PE12 8ER
Garden Building Centres	Retailing garden buildings	£25,000	Coppice Gate Lye Head Bewdley Worcs DY12 0299 266361

Global Cleaning Contracts	Office cleaning	£7,000	8–10 High Street Sutton, SM1 1HN 01–643 0146
Great Adventure Game (The)	Adult outdoor adventure game		245 Lower Richmond Rd West Richmond, London SW14 8AG 01–878 3939
Gun Point	Repointing & cleaning brickwork	£14,500	Thavies Inn House 3–4 Holborn Cir EC1N 2PL 01–353 6167
Herbal World	Retail of natural beauty products		North Eastern Chambers Station Road Harrogate 0423 525865
Highway Windscreens	Windscreen replacement	£10,000	Unity House Southend Road Woodford Green Essex 01–551 0214
Holiday Inn	Hotels	from £3 million	Windmill House 80–82 Windmill Road Brentford, TW8 0QH 01–568 8800
Hometune	Mobile car tuning service	£12,000	77 Mount Ephraim Tunbridge Wells Kent TN4 8BS 0892 510532
Hornets	Despatch service	£20,000	26 High Street Merstham, Surrey 07374 4211
House of Colour	Colour analysis consultancy	£8,000–£19,500	St Catherine's Mews, Milner St London SW3
H-Plan Fitted Bedroom Furniture	Retailers of fitted bedroom furniture	£50,000–£60,000	Dallow Road Luton LU1 1SP 0582 424222
Infopoint	Information vending	£7,500	Hanborough Bus. Park Long Hanborough Oxon 0993 881991

Intacab	Taxis and hire of cars	£80,000	West Mayne Basildon, Essex 0268 415891
Interlink	Parcel service		Portland House 22–24 Portland Square Bristol BS2 8RZ 0272 40257
In-toto	Retailer of fitted kitchens	£35,000	Wakefield Road Gildersome Leeds LS27 0QW 0532 524131
Isodan	Cavity wall insulation	£7,500	55b Colebrook Road Tunbridge Wells Kent 0892 44822
Kall-Kwik Printing	Quick printing	£60,000	Kall-Kwik House 106 Pembroke Road Ruislip Middx HA4 8NW 0895 632700
Keith Hall	Hairdressing		119–121 Derby Road Long Eaton Nottingham 0602 729914
Kentucky Fried Chicken	Chicken take-away and restaurant		Wicat House 403 London Road Camberley Surrey GU15 3HL 0276 686151
Kimberley's	Hi-fi retailers		Unit 3 Stafford Park Hornchurch, Essex
Knobs & Knockers	Retailers of brass door furniture	£40,000–£45,000	36-40 York Way London W1 01–278 8925
Kwik-Strip	Stripping and restoring furniture	£8,500	Units 1–2 306 Estate 242 Broomhill Rd Brislington Bristol 0272 772470

The Late Late Supershop	Convenience store	£75,000	PO Box 53 New Century House Manchester M60 4ES 061 834 1212
M & B Marquees	Marquee and equipment hire	£17,500	Unit 18 Swinbourne Court Burnt Hills Indus. Estate Basildon, Essex 0268 728361/ 710467
Maids (The)	Domestic cleaning	£8,000	8–10 High Street Sutton, Surrey 01–643 0138
Mainley Marines	Pet shops/ aquarium retailers	£35,000	6 Trojan Way Croydon, Surrey 01–681 8421
Master Thatchers	Roof thatching	£12,000	Rose Tree Farm 29 Nine Mile Ride Finchampstead Wokingham, Berks RG11 4QD 0734 732361
McDonalds	Hamburger restaurants		11–59 High Street East Finchley London N2 01–883 6400
Metro Rod	Drain & pipe cleaning – domestic & industrial	£30,000	Metro House Churchill Way Macclesfield Cheshire 0625 34444
Microfilm Express	Service & equipment supply centres	£40,000	Microfilm House Radley Road Abingdon, Oxon 0235 35997
Midas	Retail car repairs	£100,000	107 Mortlake High Street London SW14 8HH 01–878 7803
Millies' Cookies	Retail cookie shops	£60,000	24a Perivale Indust. Park Greenford, Middx 01–997 9793

Miximate	On-site concrete mixing	£15,000–£17,000	Bourne Way Hayes, Kent 01–462 8011
Mobiletuning	Mobile car engine tuning	£11,000	7a Nelson Road Greenwich London SE10 9JB 853 1520
Moda Biella	Retail of Italian lightweight suits		The Gianni Baldo Organisation 10 Holmstall Parade Edgware Road Edgware, Middx 01–205 3148
Molly Maid	Domestic cleaning	£5,500	10–12 Henry Road Slough, Bucks 0753 35343
Morley's	Chicken & hamburger restaurant & take-away	£140,000	162 High Street Clapham London SW4 01–622 4821
Motabitz	Wholesalers through van deliveries	£15,000	18 Church Green East Redditch, Worcs 0527 584878
Mr Clutch	Rapid clutch replacement	£24,000–£30,000	20 Lower Coombe Street Croydon, Surrey 01–686 9330
Mr Lift	Sale, hire & service of fork lift trucks	£67,500	The Lifthouse Gloucester Road Aldmondsbury Bristol 0454 618181
National Security	Installation of security systems	£2,500	Ferngreen Associates Ltd Denbigh House Denbigh Road 0908 270007
Nationwide Investigations	Private investigators	£12,500	Nationwide House 86 Southwark Bridge Road London SE1 0EX 01–928 1799

Northern Dairies	Milk delivery	£5,000	Beverley House St Stephen's Square, Hull 0482 25432
Oasis Trading	Fashion retail	£60,000	7–8 Cave Street Oxford 0865 723561
Oliver's	Coffee shop & bakery	£260,000	Eagle Court Harpur Street Bedford MK40 1JZ 0234 328181
Original Art Shop	Retail of pictures and picture framing	£30,000	12 South Church Road Southend-on-Sea Essex 0702 460391
Original Kitchen Company (The)	Design, manufacture and fitting of kitchens, bedrooms and bathrooms	£80,000	81 Calverley Road Tunbridge Wells Kent 0892 510125
Pancake Place (The)	Restaurants	£100,000	30 New Road Milnathort Kinross KY13 7XT 0577 63969
Pass & Co	Timber preservation and damp proofing	£9,780	Passco House 635 High Road Leytonstone London E11 4RD 01–539 1105
PDC Copyprint	Quick printing	£48,000	1 Church Lane East Grinstead West Sussex 0342 315321
Perfect Pizza	Take-away and pizza deliveries	£70,000–£75,000	65 Staines Road Hounslow, Middx 01–577 1711
Phone-In	Retail of telecommunication equipment	£20,000	Thomas Watson House Northumberland Street Darlington Co. Durham
PIP	Quick printing	£35,000	Black Arrow House 2 Chandos Road London

Pizza Express	Pizza restaurants	£150,000	29 Wardour Street London W1V 3HB 01–437 7215
Poppies	Domestic cleaning service	£10,730	31 Houndgate Darlington Co. Durham 0325 488699
Poppy's Body Centre	Retail of natural skin care products	£40,000	87 Skipton Road Harrogate North Yorks 0423 500206
Pops Choice	Hamburger restaurants and take-away	£65,000	25 Carfax Horsham, Sussex 0403 54630
PPG Industries	Distributors to the vehicle re-finishing trade		Rotton Park Street Birmingham 455 9866
Practical Use Car Rental	Car rental		137–145 High St Bordesley Birmingham B12 0JU 021 771 4524
Primetime Video Centre	Video rental	£50,000–£60,000	408 Manchester Road Heaton Chapel Stockport 061 431 5138
Professional Appearance Services	Car & commercial contract cleaning	£11,940	1 Queen Square Bath, Avon 0255 312756
Prontaprint	Quick printing	£75,000	Coniscliffe House Coniscliffe Road Darlington DL3 7EX 0325 483333
Pronuptia de Paris Bridal Wear	Bridal wear retail	£40,000–£80,000	Youngs Franchise Ltd
Youngs Formal Wear for Men	Formal wear hire		70–78 York Way London N1 9AG 01–278 0343
RBS Accountancy and Book-Keeping	Accountancy practice	£25,000–£40,000	Regional Business Services Ltd Regional House Troy Road, Horsforth Leeds 0532 589225

Rennbath	On-site bath renovation		226 Dyer Street Cirencester Glos 0285 66624
Rodier Paris	Ladies and gentlemen's fashions		32 Great Pulteney Street London W1R 3DE 01–437 1683
Safeclean	On-site furnishing care services	£8,500	Delmae House Home Farm Ardington Wantage Oxon OX12 8PN 0235 833022
Scotchcare Services	On-site treatment of furniture		Unit 7 Griffin Centre Feltham Middx 01–844 2222
Seeters	Estate agency	£30,000	Thornganby Ltd 200b Haverstock Hill London NW3 01–794 7194
Serviceman	Car servicing in British Rail car parks		Northgate House High Pavement Basildon, Essex 0268 293355
Servicemaster	1) On site carpet and upholstery cleaning	£10,000	50 Commercial Square Freeman's
	2) Contract cleaning	£9,000	Common Leicester LE2 7SR 0533 548620
Silver Shield Windscreens	Windscreen replacement	£20,000–£22,000	Wheler Road Coventry 0203 307755
Singer	Retailing of sewing machines		Unit H Grafton Way West Ham Industrial Estate Basingstoke RG22 6HZ 0256 56291
Sir Speedy Printing Centre	Quick printing	£68,000	28 Grays Inn Road London WC1 01–430 2332

Sketchley	Dry cleaners		PO Box 7 Rugby Road Hinckley, Leics 0455 38133
Snap-on-Tools	Automotive hand tools and equipment distributors	£36,000	Palmer House 150–154 Cross Street, Sale Cheshire M33 1AQ
Snappy Snaps	1hr film processing	£78,000	52 Notting Hill Gate London W11 01–727 6680
Snappy Tomato Pizza	Pizza take-away & delivery	£45,000	Able Foods Ltd 1 Lyon Way Greenford, Middx 01–578 5785
Spud-U-Like	Baked potato restaurant & take-away	£50,000–£60,000	34–38 Standard Road Park Royal London NW10 6EU 01–965 0182
Stained Glass Overlay	Decorative glass	£25,000	PO Box 65 Norwich NR6 6EJ 0603 485454
Stop a Thief	Car alarm fitting service	£5,000 plus vehicle	Unit 9, Avenue One Business Park Letchworth, Herts 0462 670555
Strachan Studio	Fitted bedroom furniture	£65,000	George Strachan & Co Ltd Cross Green Way Cross Green Industrial Estate Leeds 0532 495694
Swinton Insurance	Insurance brokers	£18,000	31–33 Princess Street Manchester M2 4EW 061 236 8697
Taco Time	Mexican style restaurants	£150,000	A Taste of Mexico Ltd Davidson House Green Man Lane Hatton Cross Feltham, Middx Middx 01–890 9896

Team	Wholesale distribution of audio & video equipment & accessories	£6,000	Haverscroft Indust. Estate Attleborough Norfolk 0953 454544
Thorntons	Retail of confectionery		J W Thornton Ltd Derwent Street Belper DE5 1WP 077 382 4181
Tie Rack	Retailers of ties and accessories	£30,000–£40,000	Tie Rack PLC Capital Interchange Way Brentford TW8 0EX 01–995 1344
TNT Parcel Service	Express parcel deliveries	£5,000	102 Long Street Atherstone Warks CV9 1VS 08277 5311
Town & Country Car Rental	Car rental		Harrier House 21 Yiewsley High Street West Drayton Middx 0895 441822
Trust Parts	Van sales of workshop tools	£12,500	7 Groundwell Industrial Estate Crompton Road Swindon 0793 723749
Quality International	Hotels	Variable	Piccadilly House 33 Regent Street London SW1 01–439 4955
Unigate	Distribution of milk		14–40 Victoria Road Aldershot, Hants GU1 11TH 0252 24522
Uticolour	Leather & vinyl repair process	£5,000	Sheraton House 35–37 North Street York YO1 1JD 0904 37798
VDU services	Computer cleaning	£8,350	VDU House Brook Road Wormley, Surrey 042 879 3733

Ventrolla	Installation of draught proofing systems	£16,500	51 Tower Street Harrogate North Yorks 0423 67004
Vinyl Master	Vinyl repairs and upholstery	£3,500	Unit 20 Vilcan Works 205 Leckhampton Road Cheltenham 0242 584511
West Coast Video	Video rental	£150,000	High Point Hyde Lea Stafford 0785 223447
Wetherby Training Services	Secretarial & computer training centres	£8,000	15 Victoria Street Wetherby W. Yorks LS2 4RE 0937 63940
Wimpy	Hamburger restaurants	£450,000	10 Windmill Road London W4 1SD 01–994 6454
Yves Rocher	Retail of beauty products		664 Victoria Road South Ruislip Middx HA4 0NY 01–845 1222
Ziebart	Rust proofing		Deegard Car Care Ltd 3 Downsbrook Trading Estate Southdown View Way, Worthing W. Sussex BN14 8QN 0903 212467

Full members' list
(Reproduced by kind permission of the British Franchise Association)

Franchisors are required to submit a completed application form, including disclosure document, franchise agreement, prospectus, accounts, etc., and provide proof of a correctly constituted pilot scheme successfully operated for at least one year, financed and managed by the applicant company. In addition, evidence of successful franchising over a subsequent two year period with at least four franchisees is required.

Accounting Centre (The) Elscot House Arcadia Avenue London N3 2JE	Mr I. Davies 01–349 3191	Computerised accounting services and company 'doctor' service
Alan Paul Hairdressing PLC 164 New Chester Road Birkenhead Merseyside	Mr M Rowland 051 666 1060	Ladies and gentlemen's hairdressing and retail
Alfred Marks (Franchise) Ltd Adia House 84–86 Regent Street London W1A 1AL	Mr M. Horgan 01–437 7855	Employment bureau
Alpine Soft drinks PLC Richmond Way Chelmsley Wood Birmingham B37 7TT	Mr J. Flanagan 021 770 6816	Sales of soft drinks and allied products direct to consumers at their homes
ANC Holdings Ltd Berryhill Trading Estate Victoria Road Fenton Stoke-on-Trent Staffs ST4 2NS	Mr D. L. Boon 0782 260478	Next-day national parcel freight delivery/ collection service

| **Anicare Group Services
(Veterinary) Limited**
27 Buckingham Road
Shoreham-by-Sea
Sussex BN4 5UA | Mr J. P. Sheridan
0273 63022 | Management services to
the veterinary
profession |

**Anicare Group Services
(Veterinary) Limited**
27 Buckingham Road
Shoreham-by-Sea
Sussex BN4 5UA
Mr J. P. Sheridan
0273 63022
Management services to
the veterinary
profession

Ap Autela
Autela House
PO Box No 80
Tachbrook Road
Leamington Spa
Warks CV31 3QR
Mr R. Taylor
0926 883621
Automative part
suppliers

Apollo Window Blinds Ltd
79 Johnstone Avenue
Cardonald Industrial
    Estate
Glasgow G52 4YH
Mr J. Watson
041 810 3021
Manufacturers and
retailers of window
blinds to the domestic
and commercial
markets

**Applied Motors (Europe)
    Ltd**
Victoria Wharf
Dragoon Road
London SE8 3NW
Mr J. Taylor
01–691 5921
Range of automotive
replacement parts for
VW/Audi

Avis Rent A Car Ltd
Trident House
Station Road
Hayes
Middx UB3 4DJ
Mr T. Brewer
01–848 8765
Short term car rental

Badgeman Ltd
Sketchley Business
    Services Group
PO Box 7
Rugby Road
Hinckley
Leics LE10 2NE
Mr T. A. Howarth
0453 38133
Manufacture and sale of
personalized name
badges

Bally Group (UK) Ltd
Wells House
79 Wells Street
London W1P 4JL
Mr P. W. Peters
01–631 4222
Retail shoes

**Balmforth & Partners
    (Franchises)**
St Mary's House
Duke Street
Norwich NR3 1QA
Mr A. R. Balmforth
0603 660555
Residential estate
agency

British Damp Proofing
The School House
Fleetwood Rd, Esprick
Preston PR4 3HJ
Mr B. Wainwright
039 136 441
Damp proofing/timber
treatment

Budget Rent-A-Car International Inc 41 Marlowes Hemel Hempstead Herts HP1 1LD	Keith Harman 0442 232555	National and international self-drive car, van and truck rental service
BurgerKing (UK) Ltd 20 Kew Road Richmond Surrey TW9 2NA	Mr J. Scott 01–940 6046	Fast food restaurants
City Link Transport Holdings Ltd Batavia Road Sunbury on Thames Middx TW16 5LR	Mr R. Thomas 0932 788799	Same day and overnight parcel delivery service
Clarks Shoes Ltd 40 High Street Street Som BA16 0YA	Mr P. Monaghan 0458 43131	Retail shoe shops
Coca Cola Export Corporation (The) (*Please note: no further franchises are available*)	Mr D. Rodin	Soft drinks. Contact the BFA direct for addresses of northern and southern bottlers
Colour Counsellors Ltd* 187 New King's Road Parson's Green London SW6 *particularly suitable for ladies.	Mrs V. Stourton 01–736 8326	Interior decorating. Colour catalogued samples of wallpapers, carpets and fabrics
Command Performance Intl High End Troutstream Way Loudwater Herts WD3 4LQ	Mr J. G. Macaulay Rickmansworth 0923 777636	Ladies and men's hairdressing and beauty
Computerland Europe Sarl 518 Elder House Elder Gate Central Milton Keynes Bucks	Mr C. Booth Mr S. Evans 0908 664244	Retail sale of microcomputer software and hardware
Country Rose Management (Franchise) Ltd Country Properties 6c Brand Street Hitchin Herts SG5 1HX	Mr N. J. Ramsden 0462 54040	Full estate agency service specializing in country towns, villages and rural areas

Crown Eyeglass Stancliffe Street Blackburn BB2 2QR	Mr J. Lee 0254 51535	Sale of prescription spectacles
Dampcure/Woodcure 30 Darley House Cow Lane Garston Watford Herts	Mr & Mrs J. Darley 0923 41514	Damp proofing/timber treatment
Don Millers Hot Bread Kitchens 166 Bute Street Mall Arndale Centre Luton Beds LU1 2TL	Mr M. J. B. Ward 0582 422781	Hot bread kitchens
Dyno-Services Ltd Zockoll House 143 Maple Road Surbiton Surrey KT6 4BJ	Peter Williams 01–549 9711	Drain and pipe cleaning service
Eds Drycleaning Systems Ltd Euroclean Centre 15 The Mall Heathway Dagenham Essex RM10 8RE	Mr J. Hopkinson 01–595 4234	Dry cleaning
Everett Masson & Furby Ltd 18 Walsworth Road Hitchin Herts SG4 9SP	Mr I. Littlewood 0462 32377	Business and commercial property agents
Exchange Travel (Franchises) Ltd Exchange House 66–70 Parker Road Hastings E. Sussex TN34 3UB	Mr D. Beechinor 0424 423571 Ext. 206	Travel agency
Fastframe Franchises Ltd 28 Blandford Street Sunderland SR1 3JH	Ian Johnson 091 5652233	Instant picture and related framing service
Fotofast (Terryford) Ltd 4th Floor Carolyn House 22–26 Dingwall Road Croydon CR0 9XF	Mr D. Shone 01–688 2770	Receipt and collection of films for processing and the processing of films on retail premises

Global Franchise Services 8–10 High Street Sutton Surrey SM1 1HN	Mr K. Wearn 01–642 0054	Office cleaning, contract sales and management agency

Great Adventure Game
   (The)
254 Upper Richmond
   Road West
London SW14 8AG
	Mr J. Wright
	01–878 3939
		Outdoor tactical
		adventure game for
		adults held in
		woodlands

Holiday Inns (UK) Ltd Windmill House Windmill Road Brentford Middx TW8 0QH	Mr P. M. Gee 01–568 8800	Hotels
Home Tune Ltd 77 Mount Ephraim Tunbridge Wells Kent TN4 8BS	Mr D. Collins 0892 510532	Car tuning service
Interlink Express Parcels **Ltd** Portland House 22–24 Portland Square Bristol BS2 8RZ	Mr R. Gabriel 0272 40257	Express courier parcel service
In-Toto Ltd Wakefield Road Gildersome Leeds LS27 0QW	Mr M. Eccleston 0532 524131	Retailing of kitchens and bathroom furniture, appliances and ancillary merchandise
Kall-Kwik Printing (UK) **Ltd** Kall-Kwik House 106 Pembroke Road Ruislip Middx HA4 8NW	Mr M. Gerstenhaber 08956 32700	Quick printing centres offering comprehensive design, printing, finishing and photocopying service
Keith Hall Hairdressing 2 Oxford Street Long Eaton Nottingham NG10 1JR	Mr R. B. Gosnell 0602 729914	Ladies & gents' hairdressing
Kentucky Fried Chicken **(GB) Ltd** Wicat House 403 London Road Camberley Surrey GU15 3HL	Mr P. Cox 0276 686151	Fast food

Late Late Supershop (UK) **Ltd (The)** PO Box 53 New Century House Manchester M60 4ES	Mrs J. M. Campbell 061 834 1212	Convenience store retailing
Master Thatchers Ltd Rose Tree Farm 29 Nine Mile Ride Finchampstead Wokingham Berks RG11 4QD	Mr R. C. West 0734 734203	Thatching in water reed and combed wheat reed including repairs, patching and re-ridging
Midas (Great Britain) Ltd 107 Mortlake High Street London SW14 8HH	Mr Phillips 01–878 7803	Retail exhaust system replacement
Mixamate Holdings Ltd Station Yard Bourne Way Hayes Kent BR2 7EY	Mr P. Bates 01–462 8011	Specialized concrete delivery service to builders and DIY
Mobiletuning Ltd 7a Nelson Road Greenwich London SE10 9JB	Mr A. R. Rowntree 01–853 1520	Mobile car engine- tuning service
Nationwide Investigations 86 Southwark Bridge Road London SE1 0EX	Mr K. Walker 01–928 1799	Private investigations bureau
Northern Dairies Ltd 33 Hemsworth Road Sheffield S8 8LJ	Mr D. Broomhead 0742 553563	Manufacture, processing, packaging, marketing and distribution of milk and dairy produce
Oasis Trading 7–8 Cave Street Oxford	Mr A. Thomas 0865 723561	Retail of clothing, jewellery, accessories
Olivers (UK) Ltd Eagle Court Harpur Street Bedford MK40 1JZ	Mr N. H. Allen 0234 328181	Bakery and coffee shops
PDC Copyprint **(Franchise) Ltd** 1 Church Lane East Grinstead W. Sussex RH19 3AZ	Mr M. Marks 0342 315321	Quick printing shops

PPG Industries (UK) Ltd PO Box 359 Rotton Park Street Birmingham B16 0AD	Mr D. A. V. Swanwick 121 455 9866	Distribution of paint and other products to car repair and respray garages
Pancake Place Ltd (The) Clydesdale Bank House 30 New Road Milnathort Kinross KY13 7XT	Mr R. D. Kay 0577 63969	Pancake restaurants
Pass & Co Passco House 635 High Road Leytonstone London E11 4RD	Allen Winter 01–539 1105	Timber preservation
Perfect Pizza (The) Pizza Restaurants 65 Staines Road Hounslow Middx TW3 3HW	Mr M. Clayton 01–570 2323	Restaurants and take- away units
PIP (UK) Ltd Black Arrow House 2 Chandos Road London NW10 6NF	Mr D. Waters 01–965 0700	Photocopying, instant printing, artwork and graphic communications
Pizza Express Ltd 29 Wardour Street London W1V 3HB	Mr J. Dell 01–437 7215	Pizzeria restaurants
Poppies (UK) Ltd 31 Houndgate Darlington Co Durham	Mrs S. Rorstad 0325 488699	Domestic and commercial cleaning
Practical Used Car Rental Ltd 137–145 High Street Bordesley Birmingham B12 0JU	Mr B. Agnew 021-771 4524	Practical used car rental
Prontaprint Ltd Executive Offices Coniscliffe House Darlington DL3 7EX	Mr P Stanton 0325 483333	Fast print centres incorporating artwork and design, commercial copying and business communications services
Pronuptia de Paris (Young's Franchise Ltd) 70–78 York Way King's Cross London N1 9AG	Mr L. Fielding Mr A. Henning 01–278 0343	Bridal attire retail shops. Formal wear hire service for men

Rodier Paris 32 Great Pulteney Street London W1R 3DE	Mr R. Green 01–437 1683	Fully co-ordinated range of ladies and gentlemen's fashion clothing
Safeclean International (D. G. Cook Ltd) Delmae House Home Farm Ardington Wantage Oxon OX12 8PN	Mr D. Cook 0235 833022	Hand-cleaning of carpets and upholstery. Curtain cleaning on site
Servicemaster Ltd 50 Commercial Square Freeman's Common Leicester LE2 7SR	Mrs B. Bruton 0533 548620	On-site carpet, upholstery and curtain cleaning. Fire and flood restoration, carpet treatment and repairs
Silver Shield Screens Ltd Wheler Road Seven Stars Estate Whitley Coventry CV3 4LA	Mr J. Oliver 0203 307755	24 hour mobile windscreen replacement service
Singer SDL Ltd Unit H Grafton Way West Ham Industrial Estate Basingstoke RG22 6HZ	Mr C. Burr 0256 56291	Retail and after sales service of sewing machines and other related products
Sketchley PLC Cleaning Division PO Box 7 Hinckley Leics LE10 2NE	Mr K. J. Twyman 0455 38133	Dry cleaning & shoe repairs
Snap-On-Tools Ltd Palmer House 150–154 Cross Street Sale Ches M33 1AQ	Mr M. Lancaster 061 969 0126	Distribution of automotive hand tools
Sperrings Ltd 13a Oakmount Road Chandlers Ford Southampton SO5 2LG	Mr J. R. Hunt 0703 262445	Convenience stores
Spud-U-Like Ltd 34–8 Standard Road London NW10 6EU	Mr T. Schlesinger Mr M. Porripp 01–965 0182	Fast food restaurants based on baked potatoes with large variety of fillings

Swinton Insurance Brokers Ltd 31–33 Princess Street Manchester M2 4EW	Peter Lowe 061 236 8697	Insurance brokers
Thorntons J. W. Thornton Ltd Derwent Street Belper Derbys DE5 1WP	Mr R. E. Smith 077 382 4181	Specialist chocolate and sugar confectionery
Tie Rack Ltd Capital Interchange Way Brentford Middx TW8 0EX	Mr R. Delnevo 01–995 1344	Retail neckware and accessories
TNT (UK) Ltd TNT Parcel Office TNT House 102 Long Street Atherstone Warks CV9 1VS	Ken Young 08277 5311	Collection points for guaranteed next day delivery nationwide plus European and international courier service
Unigate Dairies Ltd 14–40 Victoria Road Aldershot Hants GU1 11TH	Mr E. H. Finch 0252 24522	Distribution of milk and dairy products and soft drinks
Uticolour (Great Britain) Ltd Sheraton House 35 North Street York YO1 1JD	Mr E. Bottomley 0904 37798	Repair, recolouring and restoration of vinyl coverings
Wetherby Training Services 15 Victoria Street Wetherby W Yorks LS22 4RE	Mr D. G. Button 0937 63940	Secretarial and word processing training centres
Wimpy International Ltd 10 Windmill Road Chiswick London W4 1SD	Mr D. Lloyd- Williams 01–994 6454	Fast food
Young's Formal Wear (Young's Franchise Ltd) 70–78 York Way King's Cross London N1 9AG	Mr L. Fielding Mr A. Henning 01–278 0343	Hire and retail of mens' formal wear
Yves Rocher (London) Ltd 664 Victoria Road South Ruislip Middx HA4 0NY	Mr G. Walker 01–845 1222	Exclusive retail sale of Yves Rocher beauty products range plus beauty/sun treatments

<table>
<tr><td>Ziebart International
   Corporation
Zeegard Car Care Ltd
(UK Licensee)
3 Downsbrook Trading
   Estate
Southdown View Way
Worthing
W Sussex BN14 8QN</td><td>Mr H. Weir
0903 212467</td><td>Vehicle rust-proofing
and other car-care
services</td></tr>
</table>

Note from Director

It should be borne in mind that although franchising substantially reduces the inherent risk in a new business venture it does not automatically guarantee success.

At the same time, registration with or membership of this or any other Association does not automatically protect the member company, or his franchisee, against commercial failure.

B.F.A. Administrative Office: Franchise Chambers
                                     75a Bell Street
                                     Henley-on-Thames
                                     Oxon RG 9 2BD
                                     0491 5788049/50

British Franchise Association Register of Associates

Franchisors are required to submit a completed application form, including disclosure document, franchise agreement, prospectus, accounts, etc., and provide proof of a correctly constituted pilot scheme successfully operated for at least one year, financed and managed by the applicant company (as for Full Membership) but with evidence of successful franchising for a period of one year with at least one franchisee.

It addition, substantial companies with more than 25 company-owned outlets offering a franchise concept which is a replica of the existing business, with a separate franchise division, correctly constructed agreement, pilot scheme, prospectus and accounts but without a franchisee on station at the time of application, will also be eligible under this category.

Bath Doctor (The) Denbigh House Denbigh Road Bletchley Milton Keynes MK1 1YP	Mr M. H. Robertson 0908 270007 0908 368071	The renovation of bath-room suites
Bellina Ltd Bramford Lodge Bramford Ipswich IP8 4AZ	Mr K. C. Ball 0473 48448	Retail sale of Belgian chocolates
Berni & Host Group Ltd **(The)** Oxford House 97 Oxford Road Uxbridge UB8 1HX	Mr D. J. Mitchell 0895 70955	Franchised licensed restaurants
Britannia Business Sales **Ltd** Skyline Chambers 2nd Floor Suite 14 Manor Row Bradford W Yorks BD1 4NL	Mr J. G. Thompson 0274 722977	Licensed trade specialists/business transfer agent

Cico Chimney Linings Ltd Westleton, Saxmundham Suffolk	Mr R. J. Hadfield 0728 73608	The re-lining of domestic and industrial chimneys
Circle 'C' Stores Ltd 24 Fitzalan Road Roffey Horsham W. Sussex RH13 6AA	Mr J. Wormull 0403 61698	Convenience stores
Computa Tune 16 Aysgarth Drive Accrington Lancs BB5 6SA	Mr A. Whittaker 0254 385891	Mobile tuning and ser- vicing of motor cars
Dash Ltd PO Box 5 Rowdell Road Northolt Middx UB5 5QT	Mrs J. Sebry 01–845 7777	Retailing of fashion leisurewear
Direct Salon Services Ltd Newport Way Cannon Park Middlesbrough Cleveland TS1 5JW	Mr D. McGouran 0642 217978	Mobile van sales of hair-care and beauty products to hairdressing and beauty salons
J. Evershed & Son Ltd Eversheds Community Stores Dolphin Road Shoreham Sussex BN4 6QE	Mr P. J. Owen 0273 455555	Community grocery stores
Garden Building Centres **Ltd** Coppice Gate Lye Head, Bewdley Worcs DY12 2UX	Mr I. Jackson 0299 266361/ 266337	Sale of garden buildings, including greenhouses, summerhouses, sheds and conservatories
Gun-Point Ltd Thavies Inn House 3–4 Holborn Circus London EC1N 2PL	Mr I. Ruddlesden 01–353 6167	A mechanized repointing service for all brick and stone properties
Kimberley Hi-fi Centres Unit 3 Stafford Park Hornchurch Essex RM11 2SJ	Mrs B. Hamberger 04024 76078	Hi-fi and audio visual retailers
Knobs & Knockers **Franchising Ltd** 36-40 York Way London N1 9AB	Mr A. Newton 01–278 8925	Retail sale of brass internal and external door furniture light switches, dimmers etc.

Mainly Marines Franchising Ltd 6 Trojan Way Croydon Surrey CR0 4XL	Mr J. Driscoll 01–681 8421	Retail aquatic centres
Molly Maid 10–12 Henry Street Slough Berks SL1 2QL	Mr M. Tall 0753 77446	Residential maid cleaning service
Morley's (Fast Food) Ltd 162 Clapham High Street Clapham London SW4	Mr Peter Cavey 01–622 4821	Fast food takeaway out-lets
Mr Lift Ltd The Lifthouse Gloucester Road Bristol BS12 4HY	Mr R. Crook 0454 618181	Sale, hire and service of new and used industrial fork lift trucks
Original Artshops Ltd 28 Hemmells Laindon Essex	Mr M. Francis 0268 415822	Retail of original and reproduced pictures including instant framing
Professional Appearance Services Ltd 1 Queen Square Bath BA1 2HE	Mr D. Cook 0225 312756	Contract cleaning mainly in the automotive field and commercial premises
Scotchcare Services Ltd Unit 7 Griffin Centre Feltham Middx TW14 0HW	Mr D. M. Smith 01–844 2222	On-site Scotchguard protecting of furniture and carpets
Team Audio Ltd Haverscroft Industrial Estate New Road Attleborough Norfolk NR17 1YE	Mr D. Fossey 0953 454544	Wholesale distribution of home electronics equipment and accessories by mobile showroom
Trust Parts Ltd Unit 7 Groundwell Industrial Estate Crompton Road Swindon Wilts SN2 5AY	Mr R. Wilson 0793 723749	Van sales of workshop consumables and allied products

Solicitors for commercial enquiries

Adlers	Martin Mendelsohn	01–481 9100
22–26 Paul Street	Manzoor Inshani	
London EC2A 4JH		
Baker & McKenzie		01–242 6531
Aldwych House, Aldwych		
London WC2B 4JP		
Bird Semple & Crawford Herron	Malcolm J. Gillies	041 221 7090
249 West George Street		
Glasgow G2 4RB		
Boswell Bigmore	David Bigmore	01–353 3344
25 New Street Square		
London EC4A 3LN		
Drummond & Co.	Michael Bell	031 226 5151
31–32 Moray Place		
Edinburgh EH3 6BZ		
Field Fisher & Martineau	John Nelson-Jones	01–831 9161
Lincoln House		
296–302 High Holborn		
London WC1V 7JL		
Forsyte Kerman	R. D. Thornton	01–637 8566
79 New Cavendish Street		
London W1M 8AQ		
Ladas & Parry	Iain Baillie	01–242 5566
52–54 High Holborn		
London WC1V 6RR		
MacFarlanes	V. E. Treves	01–831 9222
10 Norwich Street		
London EC4A 1BD		
Mundays	Ray Walley	0372 67272
Speer House		
40 The Parade		
Claygate		
Esher, Surrey		

Needham & James   John H. Pratt   021 236 9701
Windsor House
Temple Row
Birmingham B2 5LF

Wm. F. Prior & Co.   C. Daw   01–353 3571
Temple Bar House
23–28 Fleet Street
London EC4Y 1AA

Owen White   Anton Bates   01–890 2836
Gavel House
90–92 High Street
Feltham
Middx TW13 4ES

Peters & Peters   Raymond Cannon   01–629 7991
2 Harewood Place
Hanover Square
London WLR 9HB

Paul Shrank & Co.   Paul Shrank   01–404 0888
7 Bell Yard
Temple Bar
Strand WC2

This list is not exhaustive and is not a recommendation.

Chartered Accountants

Arthur Young Rolls House 7 Rolls Buildings Fetter Lane London EC4A 1NH	Andy Pollock Richard Findlater	01–831 7130
Binder Hamlyn Ballantine House 168 West George Street Glasgow G2 2PT	Mr C. R. J. Foley	01–353 3020
Deloitte Haskins & Sells PO Box 90 25 Abercromby Place Edinburgh EH3 6QS	Mr M. Turner	031 557 3333
KPMG Peat Marwick McLintock 1 Puddle Dock Blackfriars London EC4V 3PD	E. S. Awty	01–236 8000
Kidsons Carlton House 31–34 Railway Street Chelmsford Essex CM1 1NJ	Mr D. V. Collins	0245 269595
Levy Gee Consultants Ltd 100 Chalk Farm Road London NW1 8EH	Mr Graham J. Woolfman	01–267 4477
Neville Russell Franchising Unit 2 Dove Street Norwich NR2 1DE	Mr K. Colman	0603 617009
M Sorskey & Co. **239 Regents Park Road** **London N3**	**Harold Sorskey**	**01–346 9361**

Spicer & Pegler   Russell Hawkes   01–480 7766
Friary Court
65 Crutched Friars
London EC3N 2NP

Stoy Hayward Associates   Mike Grunberg   01–486 5888
8 Baker Street
London W1M 1DA

The management consultancy division of Stoy Hayward, a leading firm of chartered accountants with offices throughout the UK and a member of Horwath and Horwath International. Specialists in all aspects of franchise development.

This list is not exhaustive and is not a recommendation.

Sources of finance

Bank of Scotland plc	C. M. Dow	01–925 0499
57–60 Haymarket		
London SW1Y 4QY		
Barclays Bank plc	J. S. Perkins	01–626 1567
Marketing Dept		
54 Lombard Street		
London EC3P 3AH		
Clydesdale Bank plc	A. K. Denholm	041–248 7070
PO Box 43		
30 St Vincent Place		
Glasgow G1 2HL		
Lloyds Bank plc	A. D. Pope	01–626 1500
Monument Building		
11–15 Monument Street		
London EC3R 8JU		
Midland Bank plc	Roy Manning	01–260 6379
Small Business Unit	Neil Harle	01–260 6380
120 Cannon Street		
London EC4N 6AB		
National Westminster Bank plc	P. D. Stern	01–726 1875
Franchise Section	P. A. Orrin	01–726 1920
Small Business Sector	R. L. Leach	01–726 1986
Commercial Banking Services		
8th Floor		
Finsbury Court		
101–117 Finsbury Pavement		
London EC2A 1EH		
The Royal Bank of Scotland plc	A. K. C. Auld	01–833 2121
PO Box 348		
42 Islington High Street		
London N1 8XL		
The Royal Bank of Scotland plc	R. Campbell	031 556 8555
42 St Andrew Square		
Edinburgh EH2 2YE		

TSB Scotland plc
Henry Duncan House
PO Box 177
120 George Street
Edinburgh EH2 4TS

R. G. McKie   031 225 4555

3I
91 Waterloo Road
London SE1 8XP

Jonathan Bliss   01–928 7822

Franchise trade associations

Australia	Franchisors Association of Australia Suite 7, Corporation Centre 123 Clarence Street, Sydney, NSW Australia 2000 02 29 7941
Belgium	Association Belge du Franchising 60 rue St Bernard b.1606 Bruxelles Belgium 322 537 30 60
Canada	Association of Canadian Franchisors 150 Eglinton Avenue East, 6th Floor Toronto, Ontario M4P 1E8 Canada
Denmark	Dansk Franchisegiven-Forening Pilestraede 52 DK 1112 Copenhagen K Denmark 01 13 87 67
EEC	European Franchise Federation 5 Avenue de Broqueville b.1150 Bruxelles Belgium 322 736 64 64
Eire	Irish Franchise Association 13 Frankfield Terrace Summerhill South, Cork Eire 021 270859/50
France	Federation Francaise du Franchisage 9 Bd des Italiens 75002 Paris, France (1) 42 60 00 22
Germany	Deutscher Franchise-Verband Josephspitalstrasse 14 8000 Munchen 2 West Germany

Italy	Associazione Italiana del Franchising Corso di Porta Nuova 3 Milano 20121, Italy 392 650 779
Japan	Japan Franchise Association Elsa Building, 3–13–12 Roppongi, Minato-Ku Tokyo, Japan 408 17 76
Netherlands	Nederlandse Franchise Vereniging Arubalaan 4 1213 Vg Hilversum The Netherlands 35 83 39 34
Norway	Norwegian Franchise Association Astveitskogen 41 Tertnes Bergen 5084 Norway
South Africa	South African Franchise Association Johannesburg Chamber of Commerce PB 34 Auckland Park 2006 Johannesburg, South Africa
Sweden	Swedish Franchise Association Box 26002 S–100 41 Stockholm Sweden 46 8 723 05 34
Switzerland	Swiss Franchise Association Avenue du Mail 5 CH–1205 Geneve Switzerland 022 28 36 38
United Kingdom	British Franchise Association Franchise Chambers 75a Bell Street Henley-on-Thames Oxon RG9 2BD 0491 578049/578050
USA	International Franchise Association Suite 900 1350 New York Avenue, N.W. Washington, D.C. 20005, USA 202 628–8000

Useful names and addresses

British Franchise Association, 75a Bell Street, Henley-on-Thames, Oxon
RG9 2BD 0491 578049/50
British Overseas Trade Board. Call: Department of Trade & Industry,
Support for Business Information Service 01–215 4021
Companies Registration Office, 55 City Road, London EC1 01–253 9393
The Consumers Association, 2 Marylebone Road, London NW1 4DX 01–
486 5544
Department of Employment, Small Firms and Tourism Division, Steel
House, 123 Tothill Street, London SW1 01–213 3000
Department of Trade and Industry, Ashdown House, 123 Victoria Street,
London SW1E 6RB 01–215 7877
Exhibition Organisers, Dresswell Ltd, Blenheim House, Blenheim Terrace,
London W11 01–727 1929
HM Customs & Excise, Kings Beam House, Mark Lane, London EC3 01–
283 8911
Institute of Certified Accountants, 29 Lincolns Inn Fields, London WC2
01–242 6855
Institute of Chartered Accountants, PO Box 433, Chartered Accountants
Hall, Moorgate Place, London EC2 01–628 7060
Institute of Cost and Management Accountants, 63 Portland Place, London
W1N 4AB 01–637 4716
Institute of Marketing, Moor Hall, Cookham, Berkshire SL6 9QH 06285
24922
The Law Society, 113 Chancery Lane WC2 01–242 1222
Local Enterprise Agencies (Information and counselling based on 250 local
offices, covering all aspects of starting up and running a business). Use
Yellow Pages or contact: Business in the Community 227a City Road,
London EC1V 1JU 01–253 3716
Manpower Services Commission (for details of local small business courses
and training programmes) Moorfoot, Sheffield SP1 4PQ 0742 753275
Office of Fair Trading, Field House, 15–25 Bream's Buildings, London EC4
01–242 2858
Scottish Development Agency, Small Business Division, Rosebury House,
Haymarket Terrace, Edinburgh EH12 5EZ 031 337 9595

Small Firms Service of Department of Employment (Information and direct
counselling from 12 locations nationwide including details on government
support for business) Telephone: 100 – ask for Freefone Enterprise
The Welsh Development Agency, Pearl House, Greyfriars Road, Treforest
Industrial Estate, Cardiff CF1 3XX 0222 32955

Index

pilot operations by fr'or 33, 43
Power Report 21, 42, 119, 123–4
Power Research Associates 42, 119,
    123
preferential creditors 106–7
premises/property 13, 14, 32–3, 37,
    56–7, 74, 82, 83, 85, 135
premium on lease 13–14, 34, 57
prices to customers 59, 73
private companies 98
product mix 130
profit and loss account for fr.
    operations/fr'or 47–8
profit margin on sales 50
profits/profitability 14, 15, 54, 59, 99
    judging 43
    see also gross profit
projected figures from fr'or 14, 32–
    3, 43, 44, 54, 112
promotional activites by fr'ee 73
promotional literature from fr'or
    company 46
Pronuptia 128
prospectuses from fr'or company
    45–6
public companies 98
public hearing in bankruptcy 105
Pyramid Selling 112, 117

quality control of stock 59, 72–3
questions to ask
    by banks to fr'ors 10
    by fr'ee to bank 12, 39
    by fr'ee to BFA 21, 39–40
    by fr'ee to fr'or 30–8
    by fr'ee to him/herself 30, 131
    by prospective fr'ee to established
        fr'ees 8, 38–9

receipt of money by fr'or 75
receivers 104, 105, 107–8, 109, 110
receivership liquidations 107–8,
    128–9
'recitals' in contract 81
records, keeping 93–4; *see also*
    accounts, of fr'ee
refurbishment *see* conversion/
    refurbishment of premises
regional exhibitions 120
registering companies 98
renewal of agreement 4, 36, 56, 78,
    87

rent for property 13, 34
research by fr'ee 7, 11, 12, 13, 14–
    15, 30–40, 41–54
    auditors' report 45
    balance sheet 48–9
    budget for 41
    directors' report 44
    information from fr'or 41–5; *see
        also* questions to ask
    key ratios 49–54
    principles of 54, 65
    profit and loss account 47–8
    prospectuses 45–6
    questions to ask *see* questions to
        ask
reservation of rights to fr'or 75
restraint of trade 37, 61, 70, 73–4,
    83, 91
restrictions on fr'ee 34–5; *see also*
    control of fr'ee by fr'or
return on capital employed (ROCE)
    50
risks to fr'ee 3, 30, 128–9
Royal Bank of Scotland 10–11
royalty payments 4, 6, 33, 39, 57–8,
    59–60, 70, 75, 84, 90, 112, 114,
    135

Sainsbury's 130
sale/assignment of fr.
    by fr'ee 4, 36, 60, 73, 87–8
    by fr'or 5, 36, 60–1, 78
sales/services report by fr'ee to fr'or
    70
second generation fr.s 1
second mortgages 5, 9, 30
secrecy/confidentiality by fr'ee 61,
    69, 88
seizure of goods by bailiff 103–4
selection of fr'ees 131
severance clause 65, 75–6, 92
shareholders in fr'ee company 97
Shops Act 1950 132
sites, suitable 57
sleeping partners 94
sole traders 93–4, 100–1
solicitors, commercial 29, 65, 111,
    172–3
specialist staff 38
Spencer, Cyril 128
staff *see* employees/staff of fr'ee

186

Index compiled by Peva Keane